E ...
decades. Evan was a bestsel... ...NNA CHONTAE ROSCOMÁIN
a playwright. Moreover, through his ... ...ym, Ed
McBain, he was one of the true progenitors of the modern
crime novel. He was the first American ever to receive the
Diamond Dagger, the British Crime Writers' Association's
highest award. He was also holder of the Mystery Writers of
America's prestigious Grand Master award. He died in 2005.
His website can be visited at www.edmcbain.com.

By Evan Hunter

NOVELS

The Blackboard Jungle • Second Ending • Strangers When We Meet
A Matter of Conviction • Mothers And Daughters • Buddwing
The Paper Dragon • A Horse's Head • Last Summer • Sons
Nobody Knew They Were There • Every Little Crook And Nanny
Come Winter • Streets Of Gold • The Chisholms • Love, Dad
Far From The Sea • Lizzie • Criminal Conversation • Privileged Conversation
Candyland • The Moment She Was Gone

SHORT STORY COLLECTIONS

The Jungle Kids • The Last Spin & Other Stories • Happy New Year, Herbie
The Easter Man

CHILDREN'S BOOKS

Find The Feathered Serpent • The Remarkable Harry • The Wonderful Button
Me and Mr Stenner

SCREENPLAYS

Strangers When We Meet • The Birds • Fuzz • Walk Proud

TELEPLAYS

The Chisholms • The Legend Of Walks Far Woman • Dream West

By Ed McBain

THE 87th PRECINCT NOVELS

Cop Hater • *The Mugger* • *The Pusher* • *The Con Man* • *Killer's Choice*
Killer's Payoff • *Killer's Wedge* • *Lady Killer* • *'Til Death* • *King's Ransom*
Give the Boys a Great Big Hand • *The Heckler* • *See Them Die*
Lady, Lady, I Did It! • *The Empty Hours* • *Like Love* • *Ten Plus One* • *Ax*
He Who Hesitates • *Doll* • *Eighty Million Eyes* • *Fuzz* • *Shotgun* • *Jigsaw*
Hail, Hail, the Gang's All Here • *Sadie When She Died*
Let's Hear It for the Deaf Man • *Hail to the Chief* • *Bread* • *Blood Relatives*
So Long As You Both Shall Live • *Long Time, No See* • *Calypso* • *Ghosts* • *Heat*
Ice • *Lightning* • *Eight Black Horses* • *Poison* • *Tricks* • *Kiss* • *Mischief*
And All Through the House • *Romance* • *Nocturne* • *The Big Bad City*
The Last Dance • *Money Money Money* • *Fat Ollie's Book*
The Frumious Bandersnatch • *Hark!* • *Fiddlers*

THE MATTHEW HOPE NOVELS

Goldilocks • *Rumpelstiltskin* • *Beauty & the Beast* • *Jack & the Beanstalk*
Snow White and Rose Red • *Cinderella* • *Puss in Boots*
The House That Jack Built • *Three Blind Mice* • *Mary, Mary*
There Was a Little Girl • *Gladly the Cross-Eyed Bear* • *The Last Best Hope*

OTHER NOVELS

The Sentries • *Where There's Smoke* • *Doors* • *Guns*
Another Part of the City • *Downtown* • *Driving Lessons* • *Candyland*
Alice in Jeopardy

LET'S TALK

Evan Hunter a.k.a **Ed McBain**

An Orion paperback

First published in Great Britain in 2005
by Orion
This paperback edition published in 2006
by Orion Books Ltd,
Orion House, 5 Upper St Martin's Lane,
London, WC2H 9EA

1 3 5 7 9 10 8 6 4 2

A CIP catalogue record for this book is
available from the British Library.

ISBN-13: 978-0-7528-7697-9
ISBN-10: 0-7528-7697-X

Typeset by Deltatype Ltd, Birkenhead, Merseyside

Printed in Great Britain by Clays Ltd, St Ives plc

The Orion Publishing Group's policy is to use papers that
are natural, renewable and recyclable products and
made from wood grown in sustainable forests. The logging
and manufacturing processes are expected to conform to
the environmental regulations of the country of origin.

www.orionbooks.co.uk

It is with great reluctance
that I merely dedicate this book to my wife

DRAGICA

whose name should rightfully appear
on the cover and the title page alongside mine.

But even though she wrote the many sections of this book
that are told from her viewpoint, she insists that her keen memories
and shared emotions are simply her 'feelings'.

Well, this book – and indeed my very life –
would not be what they are without those feelings.

So let me shout her byline here:

by Dragica Hunter . . .

by Dragica Hunter . . .

by Dragica Hunter . . .

(There, my darling.)

1

THE REST IS SILENCE

'WELL,' HE SAYS, 'IT CAME back cancer.'

This is honestly more surprising to me than it is shocking. I have been coping with this throat of mine for ten years now. And whereas it's become more troublesome since the summer of 2000, when Dina and I both caught colds in the South of France, we've been watching it carefully and never before has cancer seemed a frightening reality. So far, it has always been benign, benign, benign. But this is now July 2002, and Dr. David A. Slavit has just told us that the pathological report on the lesion he scraped from my right cord indicates the presence of a cancerous growth in my throat.

Dina and I are silent.

Slavit is nodding. I don't suppose any doctor gets used to telling a patient he has cancer, but Slavit seems particularly pained by the revelation now. He keeps nodding as if to confirm what he has just said, nodding as if beseeching my understanding as well; he is only the messenger, and he is sorry he has to deliver these bad tidings, but I have cancer, he is sorry, truly.

He stands perhaps five feet ten, a man in his late forties or early fifties, I would guess, though he looks much younger, looks in fact like a bespectacled, high school, science-major A-student. I can imagine him mixing chemicals in test tubes. I can imagine him as a stutterer when he was young. But *New York* magazine has chosen him as one of the best otolaryngologists in the city – an Ear, Nose and Throat man,

3

an ENT man, as they say – and he has been looking at my throat with his naked eye and with highly sophisticated machines ever since April, more than a year ago, when I was sent to him by Dr. Stanley M. Blaugrund, yet another of New York's most prominent ENT men. I completely trust both these doctors. And in Slavit's shy, intense, somewhat embarrassed way, he has just told me I have a cancer growing in my throat.

I think immediately, Dina doesn't need this!

Never mind *my* not needing it. Nobody needs it, or wants it, but here it is. My thought is that Dina has been through enough in these past seven years, she doesn't need this now. She sits beside me, my beautiful wife, holding my hand. There is a stricken look in her dark brown eyes. She is the most transparent woman I have ever met. Whatever you see in her eyes is exactly what is going on inside.

Slavit is still nodding.

I want to tell him It's okay, it's not your fault.

At the same time, I'm thinking why the hell didn't you guys catch this earlier? You've all been looking down my throat since 1992! Why didn't any of you catch this earlier?

'So what now?' I ask.

'We remove it,' he said. He is looking at me intently. He is still nodding. This is all very painful to him. I can only imagine what it is doing to Dina.

'What if we don't?' I ask.

'It will kill you.'

'When?'

'Three months? Six months? A year? But eventually it will kill you.'

'So there's no choice.'

'None, really.'

He goes on to explain that once they've removed the growth, they'll make an incision in my throat, take healthy skin from my neck, and fold this over the damaged cord.

4

'That should be enough to strengthen it and make it useful to the other, healthy cord.'

I wonder why they haven't done this earlier, *before* 'it came back cancer.' Years and years of scraping a recurring lesion from that bothersome right vocal chord, years and years of speech therapy and biopsies and, most recently, transplanting fat from my belly to the damaged right cord, plumping it up, hoping it would allow the vocal cords to close properly and bring my voice back to its normal speaking level . . .

And now – cancer.

'Can we do radiation?' Dina asks.

Although she has been in America, on and off, since 1980, my beloved wife still speaks with a Serbo-French accent. She comes from a country where patients bring a basket of figs or a roast suckling pig to the doctor whenever they visit him, but here in America she is not fearful of asking pointed questions. I am her husband, and my well-being is of far greater importance to her than any doctor's injured feelings. Besides, in the past seven short years, she's had more experience with doctors and hospitals than anyone has a right to have had. And now she wants to know – why surgery? Why not just zap the damn thing?

'We can't do that again,' Slavit says. 'Your vocal cords were radiated seven years ago.'

Yes, I think. Another attempt in the long line of futile efforts to nail this damn thing to the wall once and for all. But now it's come back cancer.

'When do we remove it?' I ask.

'In a week or so,' Slavit says. 'I'll call Dr. Blaugrund, we'll check our schedules. But first I want to make sure it hasn't spread anywhere else.'

UNTIL NOW, EVERYTHING HAS BEEN, if not casual, then

certainly relaxed. We do the biopsies, we do the pathologies, we virtually shrug when the reports come back benign each time.

But now, cancer is on the scene.

Cancer has reared its ugly head, and everything suddenly becomes rush, rush, rush.

Slavit sends me for a CT scan that very afternoon.

Dina and I taxi crosstown to a faceless building in a row of similarly anonymous buildings on First Avenue, where we enter a vast cheerless, windowless waiting room, that echoes the vast cheerless waiting rooms we've been in for the past two years, ever since we returned from our vacation in France.

In a doctor's waiting room – *any* doctor's waiting room – you wait. Now possibly, your experience has been different from mine, but I have never visited a doctor who took me into his office at the appointed hour. Never in my life. It is amazing to me that we patients don't rise up in roaring revolt, like peasants storming the Bastille. Instead, we sit there ... well, patiently. That is why we have been named patients. We are expected to sit there patiently, waiting upon the doctor's pleasure.

You will be told the doctor has been delayed in surgery – 'surgery' is one of the magic explanatory words. Or you will also be told that 'the technician is on the way,' or 'the machine has broken down,' or simply, 'the doctor is running a little late today,' or any one of a hundred other excuses for interminable delay. If it were not so tiresome, it would almost be comical.

Sitting there holding Dina's hand ...

We always hold hands.

We wait.

And wait.

And wait.

MANY WORKERS IN THE HEALTH-CARE profession become immune to what they see every day of the week. I can understand that. They don't mean to sound abrupt or impatient, but here is a sick old man or woman . . .

Even outside Medland, the old and *healthy* are more often than not treated with impatience. But here in Medland, the patient always has questions . . .

– 'How long will this take?'

– 'Did the doctor send my papers over?'

– 'Is it okay that I had breakfast this morning?'

– 'Will you make a note that I took aspirin today?'

. . . an endless barrage of questions, and the simplest way to answer them is to reply, 'Please take a seat, you'll be called.'

But . . .

We began to think we'd been forgotten. Everyone else in the room, even some people who'd arrived after us, had already been called. Dina went to check with the receptionist.

'No,' she was told, 'they know you're here, they'll call you when they're ready.'

So we waited.

And waited.

And waited.

And now everyone else was gone, and we still hadn't been called. So Dina checked again and was told to please be patient, we'd be called.

Then the receptionist went home.

And there was no one else to ask.

So we sat there waiting, and waiting, and waiting, and waiting, and hoping they wouldn't lock the doors and leave us to spend the night there, until finally someone came out and called my name.

All I could think was: I have cancer.

LATER, AS WE STROLLED UP First Avenue for dinner at a little Italian restaurant we knew on 66th Street, Dina asked if the test had been painful. I told her I'd had the usual trouble with the needle, but the scan itself was painless.

We kept assuring each other that there'd been no time for the cancer to spread, we'd only just *discovered* it! But in just three weeks it had grown from the size of a tiny pimple to a small balloon three times that size. And a week after that, the tissue had turned from a soft pink to an ugly grainy gray. We had seen this on the video screen in Slavit's office. We had seen it.

'How fast it all happened,' Dina said.

'Yes,' I said.

Was it possible it had now spread elsewhere?

'You know,' I told her, 'once this is all behind us, we still have places to go.'

We hugged and we kissed and promised each other we'd go all around the world. Not all in one trip, but for the rest of our lives, as long as we had the energy for it, we'd continue what we'd started when first we met, we'd visit beautiful places all over the world until we saw all there was to see.

If the cancer hadn't spread, that's what we would do.

ON 18 JULY, SLAVIT CALLED to tell us that the scan results were extremely hopeful. The cancer was not deeply embedded in the vocal fold tissue, it had not spread to either the neck or the lymph nodes, and there was no evidence of destruction to the cartilage.

In short, I could keep my voice box.

I had not thought I'd be losing it anyway.

So what was this?

Keep my *voice* box?

Keep my larynx?

8

What?
What!

THE LARYNX, ALSO CALLED THE voice box, is a two-inch long, tube-shaped organ in the neck. In males, the front part of the larynx is that protruding bump known as the 'Adam's Apple'. Actually, this is enlarged thyroid cartilage and is approximately the same size in girls and boys until puberty, at which time it grows larger in boys, and therefore more noticeable. The Adam's Apple has no purpose except to serve as a secondary sex characteristic. We use the larynx, however, whenever we breathe, talk, or swallow.

Here's where it's located:

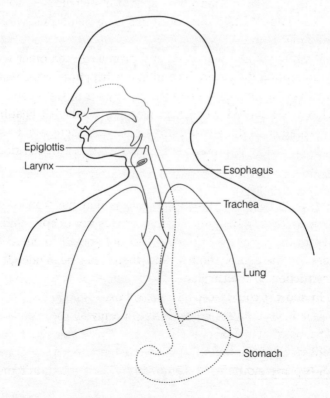

You'll notice that it sits at the top of a tube called the trachea, which leads to the lungs. Behind the larynx is another tube, the esophagus, which leads to the stomach. Whenever we swallow, the false vocal cords, or epiglottis, close over the trachea, preventing food from going down into the lungs. you remember when you were a child and choked on a kernel of popcorn? Do you remember your mother telling you that the popcorn had gone down the wrong pipe? Indeed it had. The false vocal cords hadn't closed quickly enough to block that passage to the lungs.

These vocal cords – or vocal folds, as they are also called – are actually two bands of smooth muscle tissue located in the larynx. There are the *true* vocal cords and the *false* vocal cords, the difference being that the true ones generate speech and the false ones (the epiglottis) keeps us from choking to death.

Whenever air from the lungs is forced through the true vocal cords, they vibrate and produce sound, which then passes through the throat, nose, and mouth to give each individual voice its distinctive resonant character.

Well, I'd just been told that before the CT scan indicated otherwise, having my larynx surgically removed had been a distinct possibility. Losing my vocal cords had been a distinct possibility. Losing my voice forever had been a distinct possibility.

They tell you things a little bit at a time.

This is for your own protection.

I guess.

A CT SCAN IS ALSO known as a CAT scan, but not because it's easier to say 'CAT' than it is to enunciate the separate letters 'C' and 'T'. The letters CT stand for 'Computerized Tomography'. The letters CAT stand for 'Computed Axial Tomography'. Same difference. Tomography, as if you didn't know, is an X-ray technique that photographs a single plane while eliminating the outlines of structures in other planes.

A cat is also a household pet, but that's not why a similar diagnostic test is called a PET scan. The letters PET stand for 'Positron Emission Tomography'. The color pictures a PET scan produces are capable of demonstrating pathological changes in tissue long before any other diagnostic test will reveal them. Before Slavit moved on to the next step in my treatment, he wanted to make sure there weren't any cancer cells the CAT scan would not have picked up.

So the very next day, I went crosstown to yet another medical facility, where I was injected with a mixture of radionuclide and sugar, and found myself moving slowly through another ring-like tunnel where I lay as still as a stone while the machine took pictures of my entire body.

The scan revealed that the cancer was limited to the cord's surface and had not penetrated any deeper. There was no sign that it had affected the cartilage. Neither had it spread anywhere else in the head or neck.

We had just received the equivalent of a green light from the network!

DR. STANLEY M. BLAUGRUND IS about as tall as I am, some six feet, I would guess, or perhaps even a bit taller. He has an erect bearing, a distinguished air, a neat white moustache, and a direct manner that immediately inspires confidence. I have known him for more than ten years now, since March of 1992, when I first saw him about my voice difficulties. Like Slavit, he is one of the most highly regarded ENT men in New York City. It was he, in fact, who first referred me to Slavit.

On the morning of 23 July 2002, I was once again admitted to Lenox Hill Hospital. This time, working as a team, Blaugrund and Slavit planned to surgically remove the cancerous growth from my vocal cord, and fold healthy tissue they would move from my neck onto the damaged cord. It was our combined hope and expectation that the new tissue would strengthen the long-depleted cords and allow me, at long last, to speak again in a normal voice.

Outside, Dina waited alone.

SHE TOLD ME LATER THAT she knew something was wrong the moment both doctors approached her in the waiting room. She knew what they were about to say and she didn't want to hear it. She began to cry at once.

They were both very gentle and very patient. They told her that once they were able to actually move and touch the vocal cords with instruments . . .

'Palpate the cords,' they said.

. . . they realized the cancer was much bigger than what either of the scans had shown, that in fact it had moved *under* the vocal cords as well. To remove it with a safe margin, they would have had to cut the surrounding healthy tissue as well. This made it impossible to perform the operation they'd planned to do.

'Because of what we saw,' Dr. Blaugrund said, 'we both feel the operation we'd intended would not have been a safe solution for your husband. In our opinion, only a radical laryngectomy will save his life. I'm a conservative doctor,' he said. 'We can never afford to turn our back on cancer.'

'I'm more radical in my approach,' Dr. Slavit said. 'But we agree that performing a total laryngectomy would be to Evan's advantage.'

'Then why didn't you do it now?' Dina asked.

'We need to prepare Evan for it,' Dr. Blaugrund said. 'It'll be a tremendous loss.'

'We didn't want him to wake up without a larynx,' Dr. Slavit said.

'Does he know?' Dina asked.

'I'll tell him when he wakes up,' Dr. Slavit said.

I WAS AWAKE WHEN DINA entered the Recovery Room. Slavit had already given me the bad news. Dina took my hand and began weeping softly. I was quiet, still groggy from the anesthesia. She kept holding my hand tightly.

She later told me she didn't know what she could say to me. How could she ask me to be brave when she knew I was going to lose my entire larynx, my voice box? I would never be able to speak again. My laughter would be soundless. How could she say, 'Be strong, darling,' when she knew she had no right, none whatsoever, to think she could understand the pain of such a loss?

She wanted to say, 'We can walk this road together and come out of it unchanged.' She wanted to say, 'Together, we'll survive.'

She squeezed my hand, and said only, 'I will be your laughter.'

And I heard her.

WHEN PEOPLE ASK ME WHAT my daughter does for a living, I tell them she's a drug dealer. That's because she sells pharmaceuticals for Bristol-Myers Squib.

The way I remember the name of her firm is to take one of my detective characters, Meyer Meyer, pretend he was born in Bristol, England, and further pretend he is not a cop but instead a journalist who writes fillers for the local paper. In which case one of his short news items would be called a 'Bristol Meyer's squib'. A long way round the mulberry bush, I know, but I didn't name the company, and I'm not the one who's a drug dealer.

My daughter's name is Amanda Finley. She is a tall (five-foot-eleven), strikingly beautiful woman who has inherited her mother's coal black hair and brown eyes. She is not called Amanda *Hunter* because – although she's been a part of my life since she was nine years old – I suppose she is my step-daughter. I say 'I suppose' because, believe me, she is my step-daughter in name only. In every other respect, she is as true and complete a daughter as if I'd been there to cut the umbilical cord at her birth.

Amanda has had good cause to worry about my health for the past seven years, and she is enormously concerned now about the imminent loss of my voice box. Because her sales-rep job entails making the rounds of doctors' offices, she knows some of the best ones in New York, and she informs me on the telephone that she has made an appointment for me to see a doctor named Peak Woo because if there is anyone who can save my larynx, he is the man. She gives me a phone number to call, and I speak to a woman there named Juanita – in Medland, there are many women named Juanita – who confirms my 3:45 P.M. appointment tomorrow and tells me they are on the first floor at 5 East 98th Street.

I ask if I may speak to Dr. Woo, please, and when he comes on, we have a long serious talk about whether or not he can really save my larynx. He tells me he can't possibly know for sure until he's familiarized himself with my case, and thoroughly examined me. When I come tomorrow, he wants me to bring copies of my CAT scan and PET scan reports. He wants me to bring all of the pathology reports. He wants copies of my entire case history. He wants to know everything that's been going on in my throat since 1992!

You have to understand that this is the day after both Blaugrund and Slavit discovered the cancer had spread deeply into the vocal cords and had come dangerously close to invading the lymph nodes. You have to understand that they each and both considered my condition perilous enough to warrant a total laryngectomy, already scheduled for next Tuesday morning, 30 July.

There is a long silence on the line.

I am thinking I already *have* a second opinion, don't I? With the intent purpose of saving my vocal cords, two of the best otolaryngologists in New York City – which where I come from means 'in the *world*' – have looked into my throat while I was under anesthesia, and what they saw in there, staring right up into their faces, was enough cancer to scare the living daylights out of both of them.

They have urged immediate removal of my larynx.

Not removal next month, or next year, or three years from now, but immediately, next Tuesday, the thirtieth day of July, *now*! Two excellent doctors, one older and conservative, one younger and more progressive. Both of them looking into my throat, and seeing what they saw, and rushing out to give my wife the bad news.

The silence lengthens.

At last, I tell Dr. Woo I can see no sense in keeping the appointment tomorrow.

He tells me that's up to me, of course, and wishes me good luck with the upcoming surgery.

YOU KNOW . . . LATER ON, YOU WONDER.

What if I'd got that second opinion, or a third one, or a fourth, or fifth, what if I'd sought half a dozen opinions from other doctors? Would I still have my larynx today?

I don't know.

Cancer was on the scene.

What would *you* have done?

15

TWO DAYS AFTER THE ABORTED surgery, Dina and I went to see a senior speech pathologist named Connie Kokkalakis at Manhattan Eye, Ear & Throat Hospital. MEETH as it is familiarly known, is Lenox Hill's sister hospital, and we were here in the third floor office of the Department of Communication Disorders to discuss the options open to me once my larynx was removed.

I was numb.

Dina and I were both openly crying.

She remembers it this way:

The first thing we learned was that here at the center was where Evan would learn how to talk without his larynx. There were different options: from a small electrical gadget, to what Connie Kokkalakis described as 'esophageal speech', to a more advanced and certainly more sophisticated speech with the help of a small prosthesis. We'd been told by Dr. Slavit that the prosthesis would be installed shortly after the laryngectomy healed, so I questioned now the need to learn any other forms of speech.

'It's important to learn them all,' Connie said. 'So that we'll have a backup in case the prosthesis doesn't work.'

But why shouldn't it work? I thought. It's going to be installed by one of the best doctors in New York!

I have since learned what a compassionate, loving and caring woman Connie is. But at that first meeting, I think I was somewhat taken aback by her manner. It seemed to me she was talking too loud, carefully articulating every word, as if one of us had a hearing problem. Seemingly not noticing our tears, or merely ignoring them, she moved from one subject to the next, precise and composed, glancing occasionally at her watch.

I remained silent as she demonstrated both methods of optional speech. When Evan heard the sound the so-called Electro Larynx produced, he turned to me and said, 'Darth

Vader.' Esophageal speech was even more disturbing to me. It would necessitate my husband having to gulp in air, and then belch it up as speech. This was simply too painful even to imagine. I promised myself that very minute that we would have none of it: the prosthesis would be the only viable form of speech.

Connie showed us photographs and drawings of what a stoma – the hole in the throat where the larynx once had been – would look like. She showed us samples of the different housings that would hold filters to protect the stoma and humidify the entire throat and the lungs as well. These housings could also hold a hands-free device that enabled a person to talk without ever touching the filter. She showed us samples of a cloth patch with a Velcro strap, a so-called stoma cover that would hide the stoma and its attendant apparatus.

This all seemed overwhelming. All this information was more than I could possibly retain. Looking at pictures of hollow necks with holes in them, patches of plastic pulling the skin beneath to a smooth, unwrinkled surface, listening to this young woman who conscientiously explained all the booby traps we might encounter in our efforts to find a new voice, I began thinking it had been a mistake to come here. I wasn't ready to become a member of this unfortunate group, I wasn't able to see my husband as any of the unfortunate people whose pictures we were looking at.

But we *were* these people.

Our very presence in this room confirmed the unthinkable reality of our impending future.

There was another unsettling factor during this visit: Connie constantly reminded us that the prosthesis might not work in our case, or might not be appropriate for us, or – even if it did work – might at times fail to work. There was no reassurance that once the operation was over, Evan would be able to walk out with a new voice and forget all about it. No, we would have to keep coming back here for the rest of our lives.

But Connie understood that Evan would not be having radiation after his surgery, and this improved his chances of being a good candidate for the prosthesis. As we were leaving, she gave us the card of a man who'd had the prosthetic procedure, was in fact wearing a prosthesis now, and serving as patient liaison with the center.

'You can talk to him,' she said. 'Hear how he sounds.'

LATER THAT NIGHT, HOME AGAIN in Connecticut, lying in bed holding hands, Evan said, 'This is the beginning of a downward slide for me. I'll get old, I'll die.'

I wanted to say: 'No, darling' and 'I love you, honey', but all I could do was squeeze his hand. Tears were rolling down my face, into my ears, into the wet pillow.

Dear God, I thought, what will become of us?

I WOKE UP TO AN empty bed, realized that Evan was in the studio, and went to him. I found him sitting at his computer, pulling from the internet information about laryngectomies. I sat quietly beside him, looking at the screen.

There were pictures of hollow, mutilated necks, open stomas, stomas with various housings. There were articles about the maintenance and protection of this hole in the neck, the use of various speech devices. There were letters from other people who'd been through the same ordeal, too painful for us to fully appreciate right now. The word 'Larry' was frequently used to describe a laryngectomy patient. I felt a sudden rise of anger in me, and I thought *Why do we have to mutilate even the word for it?*

What I saw was too much for me to bear.

I felt as if our beautiful life had been crushed. Our

happiness, our love, now seemed part of a past detached from us, leaving us helpless to make it our own again. *It isn't ours anymore*, I thought. We've lost it forever. Evan will never be able to laugh again. He will never, to the day he dies, ever taste the pies I bake. I can make a beautiful garden for him, but he will not smell the roses for the rest of his life.

DINA AND I HAVE CRIED for the past four days, mourning in advance the impending loss of my larynx and my voice. I've been told that when my larynx comes out, I will also lose my sense of smell and most likely my sense of taste. In a restaurant one night, I tell Dina, 'Well, I guess this is the last time I'll taste spaghetti puttanesca,' and we both begin bawling and clutch each other for support.

Tears flow at the slightest provocation.

Say 'Please pass the salt,' and we burst into tears.

THERE IS TOO MUCH PAIN; all I can do is cry.

I am not ready for the life ahead of us.

I have become an empty shell of a beloved wife, crushed by her love and the fear of losing it.

I know I am not much help to my husband.

God forgive me for this.

EVAN AND I ARE SITTING in what our architect labeled 'the great room' – a big open space consisting of kitchen, breakfast room, fireplace nook, and dining room. Large sunny windows open onto our garden, and in July the perennial beds leading to the river are lush and colorful with lilies in full bloom. Behind them the border of white flowering viburnum nestles under a service berry we planted for the birds. There is more food for them all along the river;

there are fruit-bearing bushes and the wonderfully fragrant Bay magnolias whose delicate white flowers mature into the bright red fruit that birds love. Close to our deck are the grape vines, and behind them dispersed in the garden are the cherry trees, the crab apples and the row of purple plum shading the patio at the edge of the river.

When we bought this house, Evan and I promised ourselves that we were going to make our garden a happy home for our birds, too. At our engagement party, a blue heron landed on the river to the delight of our guests. Since then, he has been the resident on our river, joined occasionally by a white heron. And so are the ducks and geese and the mama turkey with her many chicks. Our garden is now full of birds, some seasonal, some resting only for the briefest time, the others remaining with us the whole year.

I look at the rose bush.

A hummingbird approaches, its long beak sucking nectar, again and again, fluttering its wings. Last week, while I was in the garden, watering, he came to have a bath, splashing in the water, not the least intimidated by me, showing off his colorful wings, his green neck circled with a red ring. And if this splendor of color and sun in the splashing water wasn't enough, he came to my thumb, and brought his long beak to my red polished fingernail, mistaking it for a flower.

I close my eyes to the beautiful world out there and let the tears roll down my cheeks. The light breeze carries the smell of southern magnolias, and the river's murmur fills the room. The light is already fading, and we are being enclosed in the softness of dusk. We sit motionless and quiet, watching the garden dissolve in the dark, as gently and beautifully as butterflies landing.

I HAVE AVOIDED CALLING MY mother in Yugoslavia.

She has a heart condition and I'm not sure how much I can

tell her without causing her to worry excessively. There is another reason why I'm postponing giving her the bad news. It is Mom's utter delight in our happiness.

She has become used to our cheerful calls every Sunday morning. Lying in bed, we both pour out our joy over the transatlantic telephone line. Evan praises Mama for the beautiful house her daughter has made, and the wonderful cook she is. Evan asks me how to say, 'Mama, you have a beautiful daughter,' or 'What a wonderful wife your daughter is.' He writes all this down phonetically, and then takes enormous pride when Mama congratulates him on his pronunciation. This Mama of mine, who lives in a faraway village in Serbia, is as present in her daughter's life, and as familiar with her daughter's happiness as if I had never left her. In my mind I can hear her joyous laughter, see Evan's delight at knowing what a loving relationship she and I share.

On one occasion, Evan played a joke on her.

In Serbo-Croatian he had first written down phonetically and memorized, he told her in his most serious voice that her daughter had big feet. There was a dead silence on the line. He handed the phone to me. Mama immediately asked if my husband was going to divorce me. Oh yes, he might be happy with her daughter, but a man still retained the right to return damaged merchandise, a woman who had big feet! The centuries-old influence of the Ottoman Empire was still there in Mama's tiny village. It took me a full five minutes to persuade her that this was only a joke.

So how can I now tell her that Evan will have his larynx removed next week?

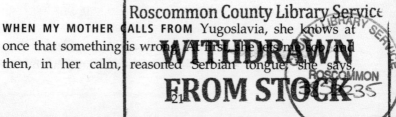

WHEN MY MOTHER CALLS FROM Yugoslavia, she knows at once that something is wrong. At first she is not sure, and then, in her calm, reasoned Serbian tongue, she says,

'Remember when I warned you to reconsider getting married to an older man? Thank God, you ignored my advice. Instead you went ahead and built a marriage your mother could only dream of. You've made me proud to have you for my daughter.'

'Evan is going to lose his voice, Mom.'

'You don't need to talk. You'll look at each other and you'll understand each other.'

'I'm hurting so much, Mom.'

'You love him and you're frightened. But when it hurts the most, remember that he's hurting even more.'

In that moment, I vow that these words will become my mantra all through the operation and the recovery; I vow that they will remain my strength forever.

I REMEMBER EXACTLY WHEN JOE Mulligan returned Evan's call. A former NYPD Bomb Squad cop, he was the man whose card Connie Kokkalakis had given us, the Voice Center's liaison with patients. It was at the end of a long desperate Friday, four days before the scheduled laryngectomy. When the phone rang, Evan picked it up and began a long conversation. There was no delay or hesitation, the conversation was flowing smoothly, they were talking back and forth. I'd been lying on the sofa in our great room, but now I sat up and began to eavesdrop. The voice coming from the receiver was audible and sounded human. Evan introduced me and handed me the receiver.

Mr. Mulligan sounded as if he had a bad cold. If I didn't know he was wearing a prosthesis, that is exactly what I would have thought. His voice sounded even, not too high and not too low, with enough tonal variety to make it sound expressive and certainly very natural. He explained that there was a limit to the volume – he couldn't really shout or whisper – but this didn't frighten us. And the really good news was that he was talking to us hands-free.

The moment after we thanked Mr. Mulligan and said goodbye, our mood shifted.

'Let's have a party,' Evan said.

DINA AND I CALLED ALL the friends we could reach and asked them to come celebrate with us that Saturday night. They all knew why they were being invited. They all knew this would be the last time they would ever hear my natural voice, such as it was; by then, it had deteriorated to a mere croak.

We set up two tables in the great room. As usual, I folded the napkins and set out the utensils and the dinnerware and the glasses. But this time, instead of chatting with Dina, I went about the task silently.

Jane Gelfman is one of the partners in the Gelfman-Schneider Literary Agency. She was my agent for a long while, and then she was no longer my agent, and then I asked her to please become my agent again, which she has been again for the past seven years. She is smart and witty and literate and savvy to the ways of publishing, and I feel blessed to have her on my side. I had told her about the cancer the moment I learned about it. It was not surprising that at 3:02 that Saturday afternoon, three days before I was to have my larynx removed, I went up alone to my studio, and sent this e-mail to her:

Dear Jane:
The potent poison quite o'er-crows my spirit:
I cannot live to hear the news from England;
But I do prophesy the election lights
On Fortinbras: he has my dying voice;
So tell him, with the occurrence, more and less,

Which have solicited.

The rest is silence.

Couldn't have said it better myself, Jane. Talk to you
next week sometime. All best, Evan

Alone at the computer, I began to weep.

In a little while, I went downstairs to pour myself a drink
and await the arrival of our party guests.

EVAN AND I LOVE PARTIES.

Here in the country, we lead quiet lives. Parties allow us to
share precious moments of warmth and joy. The first party
we had in this house was when we celebrated our engagement, eight years ago. Since then we've had parties to
celebrate anniversaries or birthdays, the arrival of a house
guest, or simply the company of good friends.

In the past, though, these parties had always been happy
events, and I could not help thinking that this time would be
different; on the phone, I'd even found myself apologizing in
advance to our friends.

THE MOOD IS JUBILANT.

None of us talk about what is about to happen to me this
coming Tuesday morning, the thirtieth day of July, the day
my life will change forever. Now, as dessert is being served,
Diane Bernhard, a dear good friend of ours, taps her wine
glass for silence, and in her delightful Texas drawl says,
'Now, Evan, we know you're going to need some help with
all those gorgeous nurses in the hospital, and we just *know*
how much Dina will appreciate our having made these flash
cards for you.'

For everyone to get a good look at it, she holds up and
shows a five-by-eight-inch, brushed-chrome box with a little

plastic window in its lid. The hand-lettered label behind the plastic insert reads:

THE SOUND OF EVAN

She sets the box on her lap, lifts the lid, and, becoming a nurse, asks, 'Did you want your rub now, dear?' And holds up a hand-lettered flash card that reads:

'PLEASE.'

'What, dear?' she asks.

I SAID, 'PLEASE'.

'Did you want a warm washcloth?'

'YES, PLEASE'.

'Is something wrong, dear?'

'I SAID A <u>WARM</u> WASHCLOTH!'

'What, dear?'

'NEVER MIND. I GOTTA GO PEE!'

And so on, for twenty or more cards that provoke laughter from all of us. Penultimately, she flashes a card that reads:

SWEET DREAMS, EVAN

... and finally one that reads:

LOVE, YOUR FRIENDS

In my gruff and husky voice, I thank them all, give Diane a big hug, and go outside where I think I'll be alone. I am weeping again when I hear a voice say, 'Evan? Come on now.'

Another good friend, Juan Flaim, is standing there in the dark, smoking a cigarette. He puts it out, comes to me, hugs me, and says, 'It will be all right.'

I nod.

'It will,' he says.

'I know.'

A little while later, C.C. Wong returns from his car, where he'd left a gift for me. He tells Dina he doesn't know whether it is appropriate to give it to me or not. He is concerned that it might offend me. The gift is a child's blackboard.

Dina and I say farewell to our friends and watch as the headlights of their cars move up and out of our driveway.

The doctors have told me that after the operation I will no longer be able to expel air through my mouth. For the last time ever, I blow out the candle in its hanging holder on a post alongside our front steps. We come inside and praise the woman who helped us serve, and then I go upstairs to my studio to write a check for her.

Jane has sent an e-mail from home.

It reads:

> For, lo! the winter is past, the rain is over and gone; the flowers appear on the earth; the time of the singing of birds is come, and the voice of the turtle is heard in our land.

I begin crying again.

I AM AT LENOX HILL again, waiting to be called into the OR. A man some ten years younger than I tells me he's been in the hospital so many times for so many different operations and procedures, that these days coming here is almost like brushing his teeth in the morning. An eighteen-year-old kid in the leather lounger next to mine tells me he's dislocated his shoulder playing football, and is here to have it adjusted. He asks me why I'm here. I tell him I'm having my larynx removed. He says, 'Oh. Right.'

When at last they come to take me to the OR, he says, 'Hey, man, good luck, huh?'

In the corridor outside, Dina gives me a final reassuring hug and kiss.

There are no tears in her eyes.

There are none in mine, either.

I KEPT WATCHING EVAN AS he walked away from me, his shoulders slightly bent in the blue hospital gown. Often, when leaving me, he would put his hand behind his back and waggle his fingers in silent farewell. He did not do that now. I watched him until at last the corridor was empty, and then I went to the waiting room.

I closed my eyes. Memories of other partings flooded over me: the silent crossing of his arms over his chest for 'I love you', the three honks of his car horn for 'See you later' and 'I'm back', whenever he drove in or out of our driveway. His voice came to me in a stream of happy memories: his loving whispers, his singing to me before we fell asleep, his phone calls from the car to keep us connected at all times, his voice overlapping mine all too often with the same thought, delighting us each time we realized we were thinking the very same thing at the very same moment.

I held these memories tight. They protected me from the fear of what was about to happen to Evan in the next few moments. I thought of the beautiful life we had, the love we'd been blessed with, a love – I often thought – that was a miracle coming so late in our lives. Enveloped by this love, I felt safe, for me and for my husband. And then a channel opened, and I began to pour my love back to Evan, putting all my concentration into reaching him, sending him all my strength. We became one again, our two lives joined again as one, our hearts beating as one heart. A sense of peace flooded over me. As long as we could share this love, nothing would ever happen to us. Evan would be safe.

I sat still and silent in the waiting room, concentrating on pouring out all my love and all my strength to him.

I AM FLAT ON MY back on a gurney, being wheeled down a long corridor to the Operating Room at Lenox Hill Hospital, smiling stupidly and bravely, and staring up at the fluorescent ceiling lights flashing by overhead.

These interior hospital corridors all look the same. They are narrow, lined with stacked wheelchairs, empty gurneys, and what appear to be discarded filing cabinets. They are the secret back passageways of ancient dungeons in Spain. Men and women in identical flapping, green, torturer's smocks rush back and forth in all directions. The harsh fluorescent lights are an overhead aurora borealis of impending dissection.

The ORs all look the same, too, and they all seem remarkably septic. One cannot imagine them being sterile. Surely, there are all sorts of crawly germs lurking in these windowless basement rooms. Have these people never heard of Joseph Lister? They are all wearing gowns and masks and latex gloves, but you have the feeling they just strolled in from some Second Avenue saloon with sawdust floors, where beer-swilling men smoke cigars, and hookers in short skirts and meshed stockings are sitting on bar stools. In this secret room now, at this concealed location, they talk about everything but you. You are not there. They are about to render you unconscious and go into your throat with sharp instruments, but you are no longer there. You are merely the inanimate object they hoist like a sack of potatoes from the hard gurney to the hard operating table. In a little while, they will insert a needle into your arm and begin the anesthesia. Someone once told you that anesthesia is the riskiest part of any surgery, but you have met the anesthesiologist for the very first time today, and now your life may depend upon how many cc's of propofol he injects into your arm. You are hooked up to machines that will register your pulse and your blood pressure and your blood oxygen level. Everyone is busy, bustling about and talking about everything under the sun but you.

The anesthesiologist starts the flow of propofol.

He asks you to count from ten to one, backwards. You get to six, and then you don't remember anything anymore.

2

THE GATHERING STORM

ON 30 OCTOBER, 1992, ON the recommendation of my internist, Dr. Ernest Atlas, I went to see an ENT man for what Atlas diagnosed as chronic *otis externa*. Also known as Swimmer's Ear, this is an infection of the outer ear canal caused by trapped water washing away the protective coating of earwax and providing a lovely wet environment in which bacteria can thrive. I had been plagued by this problem forever. In the Caribbean on vacation once, itching like crazy and seeking relief, I even went to see a man I felt certain was a witch doctor. The problem persisted.

This new doctor's name was Edward B. Gaynor, and his office was in Norwalk, Connecticut, in which town I was living with my then-wife in an old converted sawmill on the Silvermine River. I immediately begin thinking of him as Dr. Cyclops, not because he was a one-eyed giant – actually, he was a short, rotund, serious-looking man wearing a long white tunic – but because he walked around the office with a huge reflecting mirror in the center of his forehead.

On the PATIENT INFORMATION form I filled out in his reception room that day before Halloween eleven years ago, I noted that my general health was good, I was not pregnant, I had no bleeding problems, and had never suffered diabetes or hypertension. In 1989, however, I'd had a heart attack and a subsequent angioplasty – the so-called balloon procedure during which cardiologists chat amiably about the latest movie they've seen while the patient, awake, watches a tiny balloon plastering cholesterol-inspired plaque against the walls of his arteries.

My present medication included Mevacor – a cholesterol-inhibiting drug – and baby aspirin. I was not allergic to any medications. Where the form called for my smoking and drinking history, I wrote:

SMOKE AMOUNT (PAST)   *2 packs*
PRESENT   *zero*
ALCOHOL (AMOUNT)   *2 drinks*

Dr. Gaynor found none of this 'remarkable', as doctors are wont to remark. He examined my ears, nose, and throat, washed out my ears with some sort of solution, and prescribed a ten-day course of antibiotics. Then, almost casually, he asked. 'How long have you had the sore throat?'

Frankly, I didn't even realize I *had* a sore throat. It certainly didn't feel sore. Earlier that year, I'd done a whirlwind book tour that covered seven cities and some hundred or more bookshops, landing *Kiss* – the then-current 87th Precinct novel – smack in the middle of the *New York Times* bestseller list. But that had been in March, and this was October (almost November, in fact) and aside from a few local and limited speaking engagements, I hadn't been abusing my voice. In reflecting upon it, however, I admitted that perhaps I had been a little hoarse for the past month or perhaps longer.

On his chart, Gaynor scribbled what looked like *Hoarseness duration > 2 months*, and then drew a little arrow pointing to the right arm of a hand-drawn upside-down V, and scribbled what looked like *Redness esp anteriorly area? Early lesion?*

Lower down on the page, he wrote the word *smoked*, underlined it, and beneath that *3 yrs ago – 2 packs o>*.

He prescribed Beconase for the throat, advised me to rest my voice and asked me to come back in 3–4 weeks.

I NEXT SAW DR. GAYNOR on 23 November 1992. This time, in his office notes, and in his own hand, he drew another upside-down V and scribbled what looked like a dark, angry little oval close to the apex. In the margin alongside his drawing, and in his usual almost indecipherable scrawl, he wrote what looked like *Red, white area. Lesion? Endoplasia?*

Three days later, Dr. Gaynor sent a letter to my internist:

> Dear Dr. Atlas:
> Mr. Hunter returned for a follow up visit and continues to have a persistent area on the right vocal cord which is quite suspicious. We have made arrangements for him to be admitted on an ambulatory basis to Norwalk Hospital on 12/5/92 for a direct laryngoscopy and excisional biopsy of this area.
>
> Thank you again for allowing me to care for him and I will keep you appraised of our findings.

In a phone conversation with Dr. Atlas later that day, he advised me to go ahead with the biopsy Gaynor had recommended and arranged. He also told me that there was no change in my X-ray or cardiogram, that my blood work was normal, and that my cholesterol count was 213 with an HDL of 47, for a ratio of 4.5. In June, it had been 5.8. My heart problems seemed well behind me.

On 8 December 1992, I entered Norwalk Hospital for a direct microscopic suspension laryngoscopy and excision of a lesion of the larynx.

THREE DAYS AFTER THE PROCEDURE, Gaynor phoned to tell me he'd just received the hospital's pathology report.

'Good news!' he said. 'It's not cancer.'

'Good,' I said.

I suppose I felt relieved. In all truth, I never for a moment believed I might have cancer. I was sixty-six years old, and whereas that was too old for anyone to consider himself indestructible, I'd survived a serious heart attack three years ago, and here I was, wasn't I? With a low cholesterol count and a normal cardiogram, and a recent book on the *Times* bestseller list. So how could I possibly have cancer? Which I didn't have, by the way. Dr. Gaynor had just told me it wasn't cancer, hadn't he?

'It's not a tumor, either,' he said. 'There are pre-malignant changes on the vocal cord . . .'

Uh-oh, I thought.

'But these are minimal and reversible. What we had here was a moderate squamous dysplasia . . .'

'Which means what?' I asked.

'Which means an abnormal development of tissue. Pre-cancerous cells.'

'Well, did you *remove* all these pre-cancerous cells?' I asked.

'Yes,' he said.

I kept asking questions. Can they grow back at the same location? If they're all gone, what might cause them to come back again? What are the chances of pre-cancerous cells developing into malignant cells? How often will I need a checkup?

In an early January letter to Dr. Atlas, Gaynor wrote:

Mr. Hunter has done well following the excision of a left vocal cord lesion and biopsy on the right. The specimen revealed no definite carcinoma but there was atypia and moderate dysplasia. This is compatible with a diagnosis of leukoplasia which is considered to be a pre-malignant type of lesion.

In plain English, as my mother might have said, it wasn't quite cancer, but it wasn't quite normal, either.

Gaynor concluded:

However, he is no longer smoking and I think it is quite likely that his problem may be resolved. It would be best for him to be seen at periodic intervals.

Three months later, I sounded like Marlon Brando doing Vito Corleone in *The Godfather*.

A VERY LARGE DOG CAME lunging at me. I felt certain he was going to tear out my throat. A woman's voice shouted, 'No, Rex, *down!*' and the beast stopped dead in his tracks, still growling and dripping spittle. I had been told on the telephone that I could come in through the garage, the door to the basement office would be open. I had not been told that Rex or Brutus or Jaws or whatever the hell his name was would be there guarding the sacred portals. Grabbing him by the collar, his mistress dragged him out of the garage and through a door that led into what I now could see was a wood-paneled basement room. She was back a moment later, smiling apologetically, and asking me to please come in. I entered cautiously, fearful her vicious animal might still be lurking. He was nowhere in sight.

Dr. Gaynor had referred me to this 'language and oral-motor speech pathologist' for a 'complete speech evaluation' after a follow-up visit to his office on 19 March 1993 revealed 1) bi-lateral cord bowing, 2) slight vocal cord swelling, and 3) hoarse voice quality. I know I don't have to define hoarseness or swelling. The English language being what it is, however, it might be necessary to explain what 'bowing' is. To begin with, it doesn't rhyme with 'Ow!' We're not talking about the 'bowing' from the waist an actor does in response to applause. But even though it rhymes with 'Oh!', neither are we talking about the 'bowing' a concert violinist does to the strings of his instrument. The bowing here was more like a bending, as in 'bow and arrow'. In effect, the vocal cords were not meeting completely when they were closed.

You know, I think another brief anatomy lesson might be called for here. Forgive me if you know all this, but I didn't know it while everything was happening to me, and I have to assume you might not know it, either.

First, let's define the Greek or Latin names doctors are fond of using. The pharynx is the upper throat. The larynx, as you already know, is the voice box. The epiglottis, as you further know, is also known as the false vocal cords. They close over the voice box during swallowing, making sure that food goes into the stomach and not the lungs. The trachea leads to the lungs, the esophagus to the stomach.

Are you still with me?

All clear, so far?

(Oh, yes, as clear as is the summer's sun.)

When vocal cord bowing was later explained to me, I understood that it could be the result of laryngeal fracture (a busted voice box), hematoma (a blood clot), prior endoscopic surgery (like the kind I had in January), post-radiation treatment of vocal fold carcinoma (which is cancer, kids), or 'overzealous' vocal fold surgery.

I did not wish to believe that Dr. Gaynor had been overzealous in his vocal fold surgery, but given the way I sounded after a simple biopsy, it was far too easy at this stage of the game to start looking for people to blame. I now realize that Gaynor had merely been the first detective on the trail of what only much later would develop as cancer. If this had been one of my police novels, Gaynor would have been the on-duty cop who caught the initial squeal. Right now, though, sitting across from a speech pathologist in the basement office of her home on a cold blustery day toward the end of March, I couldn't help but believe that Dr. Cyclops himself was the *cause* of all my voice problems, instead of the man who'd merely discovered them. After all, I had only gone to him to have my ears cleaned!

The pathologist he'd recommended was a woman in her late thirties, I supposed, serious and dedicated, confident that she could help me bring my voice back to something approaching normalcy before the August publication of *Mischief*, the next 87th precinct novel. It was vital that come August I'd be able to conduct radio, newspaper and television interviews, do bookshop readings, and take questions from readers afterward.

The pathologist noted that my voice quality was characterized by a hoarse forced emission, what I labeled '*The Godfather* Symptom'. The hoarseness was least noticeable in the morning, but as the day progressed it intensified. She noted that to date I had not become 'aphonic' – which in simple English meant voiceless. She noted that an 'increase in loudness' (shouting, that is) improved the clarity of my voice because the vocal cords were 'forced into approximation' (forced to close completely, to touch).

She advised me not to eat chocolate (which was akin to advising me not to breathe!), and to sip decaffeinated tea at regularly spaced intervals throughout the day. She warned me against clearing my throat, which she felt was a contributing factor to the hoarseness. She cautioned me against talking in automobiles or noisy restaurants. She taught me how to breathe properly: one hand on my chest, the other on my abdomen; inhale through my nose to the count of three; exhale through my mouth to the count of three, for five minutes twice a day. She taught me how to do high-pitch counting. She taught me how to find an e-pitch, and to talk like a robot at that level. She taught me not to yell from room to room at home. She taught me to mark 'breath groups' while I read passages from my novels aloud. She taught me how to limit my talking and rest my voice.

She taught me a great many valuable things.

But on 8 August, when I boarded TWA's flight 7769 for Philadelphia to start the *Mischief* tour, the flight attendant asked me if she could get me something for my throat.

IN OCTOBER OF THAT YEAR, on the recommendation of a friend, I went to see Dr. Elliot W. Strong at the Memorial Sloan-Kettering Cancer Center.

After a physical examination confined to the head and neck area, Strong concluded that I was 'a well-developed, well-nourished, hoarse white male in no obvious acute distress.'

But clearly, I was straining my voice whenever I spoke, and whereas the right vocal cord moved normally, closure of the cords was incomplete and the quality of the voice was quite breathy.

He concluded:

'It is difficult to explain these findings in face of his history. The original surgical specimens which were received in formalin are described as being three irregular fragments, measuring 2 × 1 × 1 mm. (millimeter, or .03937 of an inch) from the left cord and one fragment less than 1 mm. in diameter from the right cord. It is also impossible to estimate how much bowing the patient had before any procedure. I presume he would benefit from an Isshiki Thyroplasty, but to what extent his voice would be returned to normal I cannot predict. He has a scheduled appointment with Dr. Clarence Sasaki at Yale in mid-November, and I have encouraged him to keep it. I have reassured him that I see no evidence of disordered growth or growth of new tissue.'

Well, it seemed clear that I didn't have cancer.

And whereas I still didn't know exactly what was going on

in my throat, I was beginning to wonder if it really mattered that I find out.

In November, Paramount Pictures – on behalf of Tom Cruise's production company – took a year's option on my new Evan Hunter novel, *Criminal Conversation*.

I almost cancelled my appointment with Dr. Sasaki.

Life was looking too good for me to be worrying about a little hoarseness of the voice.

DR. SASAKI RECOMMENDED THAT WE take a 'conservative posture' regarding my treatment, and further suggested that I begin seeing a voice therapist at Mt. Sinai Hospital in New York. It was not until May of 1994 that we realized the therapy was not working. Further examination by Sasaki revealed normal movement but 'continued irregularity of the true vocal cords.' He detected no redness, but after speaking to his associate, Dr. Gracco, he agreed that stripping of the right vocal cord might be appropriate before attempting the Isshiki Thyroplasty Dr. Strong had suggested.

On the first of June, we discussed the pros and cons of vocal cord stripping, and scheduled the procedure for one-day surgery the following week.

THE PRE-OP DIAGNOSIS WAS 'LEUKOPLAKIA'.

My medical dictionary defined this as 'formation of white spots on the mucuous membrane of the tongue or cheek. The spots are smooth, irregular in size and shape, hard, and occasionally fissured. The lesions may become malignant.'

Well, *this* leukoplakia wasn't on my tongue or cheeks, it was on my right vocal cord, and under the operating microscope it appeared to be 'slightly irregular with a small amount of keratosis involving the free edge and superior surface of the cord.' Keratosis is a tough or calloused growth.

Dr. Sasaki stripped the right vocal cord of the leukoplakia and the keratosis, and I was sent to the recovery room in satisfactory condition.

Same old, same old, right?

Wrong.

EARLY IN JANUARY OF 1995 at a Caribbean resort called Little Dix Bay, I was teamed in a Round Robin tennis match with a British stage and film director named Mike Ockrent. It happened that he was familiar with the McBain novels, and it also happened that he was a man of rare wit and exceptional good humor: within minutes, though neither of us was any great shakes as a tennis player, we had our opponents convinced that we'd once played as doubles partners at Wimbledon. At the day's end, Mike told me that he was here with a choreographer, a woman named Susan Stroman, and suggested that it might be lovely if my wife and I dined with them one night.

When I told my wife about the invitation, she said, 'What's in it for me?'

I looked at her blankly.

'He's a fan,' she said. 'He'll want to talk about you and your work, and I've heard all that before.'

'But what can I possibly tell him?' I said. 'We're here together on a small island . . .'

'I don't care what you tell him,' she said. 'The answer is no.'

I tell this story only to illustrate the state of my mind and my marriage when, later that month, I walked into the Barnes & Noble on 18th Street and Fifth Avenue.

THE LAST TIME I WAS in this store was on 28 August 1993, to do a Drop-In signing for *Mischief*. 'Drop-In' means that there have been no announcements to the public that an author will be there. You don't sit at a little table behind a stack of your books, smiling bravely and hopefully eyeing potential customers. You just put on a tie and jacket and you introduce yourself to the salesperson behind the front desk and ask to talk to the manager, who knows you're coming and who will then gather up all your books (they're called 'stock', like canned tomato soup) for you to sign in some discreet corner of the shop.

This was now seventeen months later, and I wasn't here to do any kind of signing at all. I was simply checking out bookstores that day, 'facing' McBains at the expense of other writers. When you 'face' a book, you turn it on the shelf so that the front jacket, rather than the spine, is showing. This serves as a poster to catch the eye of any browsing customer. Who will then buy the book, you hope.

On that memorable day, I had taken off my coat and draped it over a chair – I don't even remember what I was wearing that day. Given the weather, it was probably a heavy overcoat and a tweed jacket, but I can't swear to that. I was standing at the shelves, keeping an eye on my coat while facing my own books, when I heard a voice at my elbow.

'Excuse me, sir, can you tell me where to find maps and charts?'

I don't remember which book I was facing that day. I like to think it was *Romance*, the 87th Precinct title that was published that year – but I'm fairly certain that came later. This was still only January of 1995, the eleventh of January to be exact, a date I shall never forget as long as I live. A cold bleak afternoon in the city of New York. And a warm, accented voice at my elbow. *Romance* would have been an appropriate title for what was about to happen. But I don't think *Romance* was the book I had in my hands when a woman at my elbow asked where she could find 'Maps and charts', such an odd usage. I turned to her.

The woman patiently standing there had long brownish hair and eyes as dark as coal. She was wearing a long purplish fur coat. I later learned it was dyed beaver with a dyed lynx collar. Black boots added a good two inches to her height. I later learned she was five-feet seven in her bare feet. She appeared to be in her mid-thirties. I later learned she had turned forty-five in November.

'I'm sorry,' I said. 'I don't work here.'

'Oh, *I'm* sorry,' she said. 'I thought you were a sales person.'

Again, the mysterious accent. French? Russian? Indeed, in that long fur coat and high-heeled boots, she could have been an exotic creature stepping out of the snowy pages of a Tolstoi novel.

'No,' I said, 'I'm a writer.'

'I'm a drama coach,' she said, and held out her hand.

I took it.

'My name is Dina,' she said.

'My name is Evan,' I said.

Her hand was still in mine. Her dark eyes widened in surprise.

'Hunter?' she asked.

'Yes,' I said.

'So here we are,' she said.

I HAVE WRITTEN ENOUGH NOVELS to know that if you wish to gain sympathy for your married hero, you do not have him embark upon an extra-marital affair. I'd been married for twenty-two years when I first set eyes on Dragica Dimitrijevic in that bookshop on that cold January day. But I asked her if she would like to join me for a cup of coffee, and we walked crosstown and found a little shop on Third Avenue.

This was now three, three-thirty in the afternoon, cappuccino at Starbucks hadn't yet become a daily ritual for many New Yorkers. The lunch hour was over, the shop was virtually empty. I ordered coffee. She ordered tea. She told me she was familiar with all my books, had indeed read them in both English and in French while she was living in Paris, which was where she'd picked up the nickname 'Dina'.

'My mother-in-law couldn't pronounce Dragica,' she said. 'So she called me Dina. I used to take notes on your novels, you know. I still have the notebooks.'

Thinking I'd *really* impress her, I said, 'You know, I'm *also* Ed McBain.'

By that time – despite the wild success of *The Blackboard Jungle* and the Hitchcock movie *The Birds*, for which I'd written the screenplay – I was better known by the McBain pseudonym than by the name I'd legally adopted in 1952. Book a table as Ed McBain, the *maitre d'* would trip all over himself and the beaming chef would come out of the kitchen with a novel to sign. Book it as Evan Hunter, I would be seated near a telephone booth or the men's room. I waited for knowledge to dawn on her face, waited for those luminous dark eyes to spark with recognition.

'Who?' she asked.

I learned over coffee that afternoon that she'd been born in what was then Yugoslavia, in a little village named Glavica, where her mother and her twin brother still lived and tended a chicken farm. She told me that in Serbian, Dragica meant 'precious darling', though she was the runt of the litter and a girl besides, and the doctor advised her mother to throw her in the river because she would not have enough milk to nurse two infants. Instead, her grandmother carried her from house to house in this village of three hundred people, asking from gate to gate if there was a nursing mother within, begging for milk to keep tiny Dragica alive.

'Tell me how you say your name again.'

'Dragica,' she said, and shrugged aside the difficult pronunciation.

I thought for a moment.

Then I asked myself out loud, 'Shall I lift it, sir, or push it, sir?' And I answered myself, 'No, just *drag* it, sir.'

'Well,' she said, laughing, 'I suppose that's close.'

'And your last name? How do you pronounce that?'

'Dimitrijevic,' she said, again shrugging at the utter simplicity of it all.

I thought again.

'Shall I give you *one* of each or *two* of each?' I asked. 'No,' I answered, 'please dim'me *t'ree* of itch.'

She laughed again.

She told me many things about herself that afternoon.

She told me that she'd left home at the age of eighteen, against her father's express wishes, to study economics and tourism in Dubrovnik. From there, she'd gone to Paris when she turned twenty-one. Learning French, commuting back and forth to Yugoslavia to take her university exams, she eventually received her degree and met the French actor-director who would later become her husband.

On his behalf, and because her English was better than his, she came to America in 1980, to plead his case for admission to the Actors Studio. Anna Strasberg interviewed her. While Dina was telling her what a wonderful actor and director Luc was, Lee Strasberg quietly entered the room. Unseen by her, he leaned against the wall near the door, his arms folded across his chest, and stood listening to her every word. When she finished her impassioned case for her husband's admission, he asked simply, 'And what about you?'

Now, in a coffee shop on Third Avenue, in the dead of winter almost fifteen years later, she gripped the edge of the table as she had done on that morning long ago, and her dark eyes welled with tears again. She had been raised by a repressive father in a restrictive Serbian household. A life in the theater was beyond her wildest expectations.

'Put her in my morning class,' Lee said.

She told me that she was studying in Lee's private class when he died two years later. She went back to Paris to try to rescue her faltering marriage, and when the attempt failed, she divorced Luc and came back to New York to renew classes with Irma Sandrey, who had studied and worked with Lee for thirty years, and who was then the principal instructor at the Strasberg Institute. In the fall of 1988, Anna asked Dina if she would like to teach for them in their newly opened London school.

'I worked in London for a year,' she told me, 'and then came back to teach at the Institute here in New York.'

'Are you still teaching there?' I asked.

'No. I'm giving private lessons now. I had my own theater for a while, you see . . .'

'Oh?'

'Yes,' she said. 'I produced nine plays, directed five of them, and acted in three of them. On March twenty-fourth last year, I achieved Not-For-Profit Status,' she said, remembering the date exactly, nodding proudly. 'But at the same time, I was teaching Institute classes and NYU classes, and it got to be too much. So now I just teach at this little studio I rent. As I said, I'm a drama coach.'

She nodded again, lifted her teacup, sipped at it, and smiled at me across the small round table.

'And you?' she said. 'Tell me about you.'

'Well . . . you've read my books,' I said.

'Yes?'

'So you know me.'

There was a silence at the table.

'Dina,' I said, 'I'm married.'

'Yes, I know,' she said. 'I saw the ring.'

IN A NOVEL, ANOTHER GOOD way to lose sympathy for your lead character is to make him a sixty-eight-year-old man who after twenty-two years of marriage falls in love with a woman twenty-three years his junior. When the movie *Eyes Wide Shut* opened, Mike Ockrent, who was then fifty-three, described it to me as 'An old man's wonk.'

Well, maybe so.

But I met the love of my life when I was sixty-eight.

So shoot me.

I DON'T REMEMBER HOW OR by whom I was referred to Dr. Stanley M. Blaugrund, but I do remember that he encouraged immediate trust. In my Vito Corleone voice, I told him my sad tale of woe.

By that time, Dr. Strong and Dr. Sasaki had both agreed on the same symptoms: dysphonia (which means 'difficulty producing speech'), atrophy and bowing of the right vocal cord, and either redness or whiteness on that same cord. Dr. Blaugrund concurred.

There was nothing new.

But after seeing me on several occasions subsequent to that first visit, he once again noted a white membrane growing on the right vocal cord. When this 'lesion' – as he referred to it when he spoke to me on the phone – did not improve on administration of Prednisone, he considered it suspicious enough for him to suggest yet another direct laryngoscopy.

THE MICROSCOPIC DIAGNOSIS OF MY right vocal cord revealed 'necrotic debris and acute inflammatory exudate consistent with an ulcer'. It revealed 'squamous mucosa showing focal atypia with hyperplasia and parketosis'. It also revealed chronic inflammation, the only two words I understood.

But after all the medical gobbledygook, the report concluded with the words: 'no evidence of malignancy on the four levels examined.'

And that was good enough for Dr. Blaugrund to recommend going back to Dr. Sasaki at Yale, for an Isshiki Thyroplasty that he was hopeful would correct my atrophied right cord and give me a more stable voice with increased intensity.

THE ISSHIKI THYROPLASTY IS NOT the title of a Robert Ludlum novel. It is, instead, a surgical procedure named after Dr. Nobuhiko Isshiki, who first developed it. Paralysis, scarring, atrophy, all can deprive the vocal folds of either their normal mobility or bulk. The Isshiki Thyroplasty is used to correct any problem that hampers the efficient performance of the body's speech mechanism. Also known as medialization laryngoplasty (I like the Ludlumesque title better), the procedure is most commonly called a *thyro*plasty rather than a *laryngo*plasty because it's performed through a hole in the thyroid cartilage.

What they do is inject a local anesthetic an hour before surgery, and then they cut a tiny window – 0.30 × 0.15 inch in a male, 0.27 × 0.12 inch in a female – in the thyroid cartilage. Into this window they insert a synthetic implant which serves to normalize the damaged vocal folds. Because the anesthesia is merely local, the patient can talk during the entire procedure, and this allows the surgeon to fine-tune the voice as he goes along.

It sounded like an ideal solution to my problem.

But before Dr. Sasaki could perform the procedure, I went to Blaugrund for a follow-up visit, and guess what?

The lesion was back again.

WELL, NOW, THIS WAS STARTING to be a pain in the ass. It was also starting to be serious enough, in Dr. Blaugrund's view, to warrant his suggesting what he called 'a potent method of treating a benign disease.'

There was no question but that the lesion he'd removed from my vocal cord at the beginning of May was benign. But now, a mere three weeks later, it was back again.

What he was suggesting was radiation.

'I thought I didn't have cancer,' I said.

'You don't.'

'So why radiation?'

'Because I think it may solve what's been a continuing problem for you.'

I was full of questions.

'Have you recommended this to other patients?'

'Yes,' he said. 'And in most cases, the voice was markedly improved after radiation.'

'How difficult is it?'

'Not difficult at all. The radiologist will decide the frequency and the dosage. But usually, it's every day for a month or so, and you'll be under the machine for about a minute each time.'

'Can I have this done in Norwalk?'

'I'd rather you did it in New York,' he said. 'I would prefer that a top man did it.'

I was to realize only later that geographical imperative is prevalent in Medland. Ask any doctor in Norwalk where the best radiologists in the field are, and he'll invariably answer, 'Right here in Connecticut.' If you're talking to a vascular surgeon in Cleveland, he'll tell you that's where the best people in the field are. I should not have been surprised when Blaugrund recommended a radiologist at Beth Israel Hospital in downtown New York.

'Why not just go ahead with the thyroplasty now?' I asked. 'Get it over with.'

'Because if an implant is in place and the lesion returns, we won't be able to remove it. And next time, it might be malignant. It's not cancerous yet, it's simply pre-malignant. But if it turns malignant, it will be much harder to treat.'

'What are the risks of radiation?'

'None.'

'Will there be pain involved?'

'No.'

I suppose I was still looking dubious. Radiation was for people who already *had* cancer, wasn't it? So yes, this *was* an admittedly potent method of treating a benign disease. In which case, why do it?

'Would you like to talk to another of my patients who had similar voice problems, and who underwent radiation?'

'Yes,' I said at once.

ROBERT SHERMAN SOUNDED TERRIFIC ON the telephone.

He told me that before he began radiation therapy, he could hardly talk at all. He told me that radiation cured him completely. The growth on his vocal cords never came back, and now he went to see Blaugrund for a checkup only once every six months.

'The first day you go in, they do a simulation,' he told me. 'The actual treatment starts several days later. I had thirty treatments in all. No more than a minute each time.'

I could almost see him grinning as he added, 'It was nothing at all.'

*

THIS WAS NOW MAY OF 1995.

Tom Cruise and Paramount Pictures had just renewed the movie option on *Criminal Conversation*. A year earlier, to coincide with publication of the book, I had agreed to do a talk at Marymount College in New York. Before I began speaking, I apologized for the condition of my rapidly deteriorating voice, which I blamed on laryngitis. One member of the audience didn't buy this explanation. He came up to me after the talk, and said in a clear, resonant voice, 'I had the same problem. We fixed it with radiation.'

So now, on the first day of June, a year and a bit more after that speaking engagement, I was sitting in the office of Dr. Nemetallah A. Ghossein at Beth Israel's Department of Radiation Onconology. Ghossein was Egyptian, a genial man who fastened his dark eyes on me, and told me in lightly accented English that despite the fact that his examination of my larynx had revealed a three-millimeter whitish area on the right vocal cord, there was no definite proof of invasion.

'As you may know,' he said, 'these lesions may be invasive, but the invasiveness is difficult to document as frankly carcinoma after a few recurrences. However . . .'

He patted my hand to stress what he was about to say.

'Repeated surgery for recurrence will only cause further distortion of the larynx and increased deterioration of your voice. I believe you are a candidate for radiotherapy, and I would like to suggest as much to Dr. Blaugrund.'

He smiled suddenly.

'The local control rate is very high, you know,' he said reassuringly. 'Your voice should be quite acceptable after this course of treatment.'

On 9 June I visited Ghossein again and told him I'd decided to go ahead with the radiation.

On 11 June my wife and I separated and I began looking for an apartment in New York.

On 15 June I began the six-week course of radiotherapy.

And on 18 June, I moved into a studio apartment in Dina's building on the Upper East Side.

DINA HAD ASKED HER DOORMAN if he knew of any apartments for rent in the building. He told her that apartment 17C had just come free, and that its owner would probably be happy to sublet it again. When she later spoke to the owner, he didn't seem too thrilled by the prospect of renting to a 'writer'. Seemingly, he considered my occupation something akin to a troubadour, a minstrel, or a wandering gypsy. She explained that I was financially solvent, was in fact somewhat well-known, but he'd never heard of either Hunter or McBain, and remained unconvinced. Apparently, his last tenant had quit the apartment without notice, leaving him in the hole for a month's overdue rent. When Dina told him she would write her own check for my first month's rent, he finally relented.

The apartment was smaller than even one section of my studio on the Silvermine River. Furnished in Second Avenue Thrift-Shop, hung with paintings bought by the yard on Sixth Avenue, one could understand why its owner was wary of renting to anyone who called himself a 'writer'. But there was a dining-room table. And there was a bed. And there were windows fronting the avenue far below. Unfortunately, the avenue carried some of the heaviest traffic in the city of New York. When I called to tell my daughter I had just dragged the dining-room table over to the windows and placed my computer on it, she listened to the din for a moment, and then asked, 'Where are you? Downtown Beirut?'

Half an hour later, Dina came in, followed by two handymen carrying the desk from her own sixth-floor apartment.

'A writer shouldn't have to work on a dining-room table,' she said.

Two days later, she found the money.

EVERY WEEKDAY MORNING AT EIGHT, I now walked over to First Avenue to catch a bus downtown to Beth Israel on 16th Street. My scheduled appointment was at nine-fifteen and I was usually back in the apartment by ten-thirty or a bit after.

I have to tell you, I am neither a team-player nor a joiner. I had chosen a profession in which I work alone, and on those occasions when I had to collaborate with others – directors and/or actors while doing a movie or a play – I had never felt truly comfortable. Neither did I feel comfortable with the patients in the waiting room of Beth Israel's Department of Radiation Onconology. In fact, I felt somewhat superior to them. These people were cancer patients. I was not. Sitting there on a bench with men who had prostate cancer or women who had breast cancer, I felt removed and distant. I did not have cancer and I did not want to be one of them. I did not wish to join their exclusive little club. I could smile and joke with them, yes, but I was not one of them. I was undertaking radiation therapy merely as a preventive measure. I did not have cancer.

However . . .

I met my first Girl in a Scarf in that waiting room.

She was a woman, of course, in her late twenties or early thirties, but I was sixty-eight years old, and to me she was still a girl. I have subsequently met many of these women wearing headscarves to hide the baldness beneath but to me they will always seem like girls, always young, always beautiful. The Girl in a Scarf can be twenty to forty; rarely is she older. She can be white, or black, or Latina or Chinese. She can be anyone of any race or creed.

The Girl in a Scarf has cancer.

She has had chemotherapy in an attempt to poison the cancer.

She has lost her hair during the treatment.

And she is now trying radiation therapy in a further attempt to kill this ravenous beast.

In Ghossein's waiting room, we struck up a conversation. She told me why she was there. I told her why I was there. She said I was lucky.

And then, touching the brightly colored scarf around her head, she said, 'Then again, my mother always wanted a boy.'

And I said, 'Miss, there is no way you will ever be mistaken for a boy.'

And the Girl in a Scarf smiled radiantly.

EACH WEEKDAY MORNING, GHOSSEIN AND a technician would carefully position the cone of the radiation machine over the tattooed dot that located my vocal cords –

'A little bit lower,' he would tell the technician. 'A bit to the left,' he would say. 'No, more to the right. That's it. A bit higher. Lower. There, there, that's it!' and then leaning in close to my ear, he would whisper, 'Forgive me, I am very fussy.'

And I would think *Yes, be fussy, please, these are my vocal cords we're zapping*.

Ever since I'd moved into my tiny noisy apartment, Dina and I had been cleaning and tidying up the place, and it was now in almost spotless condition. That morning, while I was under the cone of the radiation machine, Dina found a pile of dirty towels and old rags on a shelf in the apartment's sole closet. Thinking she had at last reached the end of the house-cleaning task, she tossed the rags into a bucket earmarked for the garbage, loaded the dirty towels into a plastic laundry basket, and carried them down to the washing machines in the basement.

She threw the towels in, started the water flowing, waited for the machine to fill, and was about to shake in the detergent when something green caught her eye. She leaned in closer. The towels were billowing up with the rush of water. A hundred-dollar bill had just floated to the surface. She plucked it out of the water, and as she continued to watch, astonished, more and more bills came floating free of the towels. She looked around nervously. She was alone in the basement. She kept plucking hundred-dollar bills out of the water. Ten minutes later, when she counted them in my apartment, there were eighty of them. She had just almost laundered $8000!

Spreading them on the bed to dry, it suddenly occurred to her that the old rags in the bucket had also been on that closet shelf. She went into the tiny kitchen alcove, reached into the bucket, shook out the rags, and was somehow not surprised when a rubber-banded stack of hundred dollar bills fell free. She took off the rubber band and counted the bills. There were ninety of them. She now had $17,000 more than she'd had when she kissed me goodbye earlier that morning.

THE FIRST THING I DID was call the owner of the apartment.

He had never met me, and had trouble recalling my name at first, but when I told him I was the writer who was renting his apartment . . .

'Ah, yes, the writer,' he said knowingly, and somewhat suspiciously. And then, immediately, 'What's the trouble?'

I told him there was no trouble, I merely needed a forwarding address for the man who'd rented the apartment before me.

'Try Singapore,' he said. 'He probably went back there. Why do you need his address?'

'He left some things here,' I said.

Seventeen *thousand* things, I thought.

'I don't have a forwarding address,' he told me. 'The son of a bitch left in the middle of the night, like the thief he is. He owed me a month's rent. If I knew where he was, I'd have him arrested. What things?'

'Some socks and a shirt,' I said.

'Burn them,' he advised, and hung up.

Clearly, the owner of the apartment was not a man who would leave $17,000 wrapped in dirty towels and old rags for any of his vagabond tenants to find. Dina checked with the doorman again, to see if he might have a clue to the previous tenant's name or whereabouts. The doorman told her the man was trouble from the very minute he began subletting in March. People coming and going at all hours of the day or night, most of them women, tenants complaining about the noise and the loud music. He was here only a month, disappeared in the middle of April.

'Why?' the doorman wanted to know.

'Just curious,' Dina said.

WE FIGURED THE LAST TENANT of the apartment was a drug dealer who'd left his ill-gotten gains behind when he'd left in a hurry. Convinced now that we were in possession of stolen or otherwise illegally obtained cash, I suggested that we call Richard Condon, a man I'd met when he was still a police sergeant at the First Precinct on Ericsson Place in New York. Until just recently, Dick had been Police Commissioner of New York. Over the years, whenever I needed technical information for the Eight-Seven novels, he had helped me whenever I called.

Listening carefully now, he kept repeating, 'Uh-huh, uh-huh,' until I realized he thought I was trying out another plot on him. I told him I was quite serious; Dina and I were now in possession of $17,000 she'd found in a pile of old rags and dirty towels in my apartment. What should we do?

'Call Barbara,' he suggested. 'She'll find out if the bills are either dirty or fake.'

'Barbara' was Barbara Jones, who is now a federal district court judge, but who was then an assistant D.A. downtown. She suggested that I turn the bills over to the Treasury Department, and the next day a pair of agents dropped by to count the bills, mark down the serial numbers, and give me a receipt for $17,000. They told me they'd get back to me as soon as they'd run the bills through the system. I'm a native New Yorker; I figured *Goodbye, $17,000.*

Two days later, I got a call from one of the agents.

The bills were real.

And they hadn't been stolen.

'When can I bring them back to you?' he asked.

He came by with the bills later that day. He counted them out for me. Seventeen thousand bucks. He asked me to sign a receipt for them. I did.

When I asked him what I should do with them now, he said, 'Whatever you wish, pal. You found them, they're yours.'

When I asked my accountant if I had to report the money as income, he said, 'It isn't income. And you didn't win it, either. You found it.'

Dina argued that the money was rightfully mine, since she'd found it in a closet in my apartment.

I said, 'Ah, but *you're* the one who found it. The money is yours.'

She finally accepted it. In the last season of operating her theater, she had borrowed money and had hocked all her jewelry, just to keep afloat. She now paid off her debts and reclaimed her jewelry, and that Saturday night, she took me to the River Café for dinner. We sat looking out at the twinkling lights on the Brooklyn shore as we ate caviar and drank champagne and toasted our amazing good fortune and the start of our new life together.

This was now the twenty-fourth day of June.

I had been croaking my way through a faltering marriage and an erratic career for almost two years and eight months.

But on 1 August, Dr. Ghossein wrote this letter to Dr. Blaugrund:

Dear Stanley:

Mr. Hunter has completed his course of external radiotherapy for recurrent hyperplasia and perakeratosis involving the right vocal cord.

He received to the larynx by laryngeal portals measuring 5×5 cm, 6200 cGy in 31 fractions in 42 days between 6/15/95 and 7/27/95 using the Cobalt Unit.

Mr. Hunter tolerated the treatment quite well with no significant radiation reaction.

At the completion of radiation there was minimal hoarseness. On an indirect laryngoscopy there was no significant mucosal abnormality. He is now referred back to you. He was given a follow-up appointment in about a month to check on his radiation reactions.

Thank you again for referring this patient to me.

Sincerely,

N.A. Ghossein, M.D.

A few weeks after that, my voice came back.

3

EVERYTHING'S COMING UP ROSES

I'M A FAST WRITER. IN America, writing fast is considered suspect. You can write fast and *lousy* and get a lot of fame and money for it, but if you write fast and *well*, something funny must be going on. Maybe you have six chimps in the basement, doing the work for you.

During the time I got my voice back in July of 1995, and the time Dina and I started truly living together less than a year later, I had written:

Privileged Conversation, an Evan Hunter novel about a psychiatrist dealing with obsessive-compulsive patients who himself becomes obsessed with a seriously disturbed dancer in *Cats*.

A memoir titled *Me and Hitch*, about working with Alfred Hitchcock on *The Birds* and *Marnie*.

Nocturne, the forty-seventh novel in the continuing 87th Precinct series.

And *Driving Lessons*, a stand-alone novella for Otto Penzler's newly launched 'Criminal Records' series.

If I may, a few interesting sidelights about these titles.

I got a call from one of the women who'd earlier been a good friend but who had recently advised my wife to go for the jugular. She had just red *Priv Con*. She gushed, 'Oh, Evan, *now* I understand!'

'What is it you understand?' I asked.

'It's all right,' she assured me. 'I understand.'

Word had been circulating that I'd fallen madly in love with a nutty dancer from *Cats*! This woman was calling to tell

63

me it was okay by her since I myself was most likely certifiable.

Regarding the Hitchcock memoir. On the *Crim Con* tour, while I was doing a radio show with Bob Slade at New York's WRKS, he asked me about my experience working with Hitch, and I went on about it at some length. When we left the studio, Patricia Keim, who was then the publicist at Warner Books, suggested that I write a short piece about Hitch, which she would then try to place with one of the newspapers. The 'short' piece turned out to be eighty manuscript pages! Patricia never sent it to any of the papers, but I later sold it to Faber & Faber, and the book is dedicated to her. (Incidentally, because I was still alive and Hitch wasn't, I gave myself top billing in the title.)

I wrote *Nocturne* at Dina's desk in my windfall apartment, with the windows open to the incessant traffic below. One of the scenes in the novel has a man coming down from his apartment to shoot a taxi driver honking his horn. Meyer Meyer, the detective arresting him, considers it justifiable homicide.

Driving Lessons was told from the viewpoint of a female detective whose husband has left her for a much younger woman.

Talk about feelings of guilt.

'YOU DON'T EVEN *SOUND* LIKE yourself anymore!' my wife told me on the telephone. This was supposed to be a reprimand. I considered it a compliment. She had grown so accustomed to my Vito Corleone imitation that she'd forgotten what the original Evan Hunter sounded like. By this time, I was desperately wishing she'd forget what the original Evan Hunter *looked* like as well. I don't know how many of you have been through divorces, but my advice to those of you who haven't is this: If you don't have to get one, don't.

(I would say the same thing about cancer of the larynx, by the way. If you don't have to get it, don't.)

I cannot begin to tell you how many of the women I considered mutual friends now began advising my wife to 'take the son of a bitch to the cleaners.' Women who'd laughed at my jokes and eaten at my table were now recommending killer divorce lawyers who would cut off my balls. My male friends took a different tack. One after the other, they asked me to have lunch with them, and one after the other, with little locker-room nudges of the elbow, they intimated that they themselves had enjoyed little flings during the course of their sometimes stormy marriages. But hey, look, kiddo, enjoy yourself, and then go back home, okay? Don't be a fool, don't throw away everything you've built over the years. You've got a gem there, kiddo, and she still loves you. Be smart about this, hm?

And a wink.

The gem who still loved me had hired a New York divorce lawyer renowned for his surgical skills. Until now, I hadn't realized I was a 'celebrity'. Now I was being warned that if I didn't come to a settlement soon, my marital problems would be spread all over the front page of the *Daily News*. Did I want my millions (ha!) of readers to learn that I was playing around with some kind of foreigner while my wife of twenty-two years wept alone in our riverbank hovel?

By then, I had rented a furnished house on Charcoal Hill in Westport, Connecticut. While Dina came up to visit me on weekends, my weeping wife of twenty-two years continued to throw lavish parties in the luxurious Silvermine house we still jointly owned. My son and his wife attended those parties. So did my daughter. And all my friends. It was as if I were away on an extended book-tour. Business as usual. Chatter, chatter, chatter. But nobody talked about The Bimbo.

Dragica Dimitrijevic simply didn't exist.

Except in my heart.

Except in my thoughts every moment of every single day.

DINA REMEMBERS IT THIS WAY:

The house on Charcoal Hill was Evan's place. He said he was renting it so that he could work in an atmosphere quieter than the one in the New York studio apartment. But that apartment was only eleven floors above my own, and I now felt a sense of rupture, even though I knew I'd be visiting him every weekend.

We moved only cautiously into the future.

Evan began to introduce me to a carefully chosen group of friends. He began teaching me how to drive, so that I could become more independent. Gradually, my weekend visits became longer, and soon we stopped worrying about which restaurant we'd go to, or by whom we'd be seen when we were out together. Our decision to stay together forever came as naturally as our love had come to us. We put up our first Christmas tree, and booked a trip to the Caribbean. By the time we left to celebrate the new year at the K-Club, we were as one person.

I FELT NO GUILT.

In fact, I felt great.

I had found the woman with whom I planned to spend the rest of my life.

I was writing fast and writing well.

And if I needed any confirmation that the problems with my voice were a thing of the past, I had just taped the audio version of *Privileged Conversation* without a single glitch.

Moreover . . .

December 7, 1995

Dr. Stanley Blaugrund
151 E. 61st St.
New York, NY 10021

Re: Hunter, Evan
RT #94–26–69
MR #132 94 48

Dear Stanley:

I saw today Mr. Hunter who is now five months after completion of radiotherapy for a hyperplasia of the right vocal cords. He is doing quite well and has no significant hoarseness.

On direct laryngoscopy, I do not identify any lesion in the extrinsic or intrinsic larynx and both vocal cords are mobile. There are no significant post radiation changes and only minimal edema of the arytenoid.

I understand that you are following him regularly and have given him an appointment for six months.

Sincerely yours,

N.A. Ghossein, M.D.

THE MAN ON THE TELEPHONE identified himself as Timothy Childs. He told me he was a Broadway producer who had optioned the rights to a book and subsequent motion picture titled *The Night They Raided Minsky's*, and asked if I would be at all interested in writing the book for a musical based on the property.

For those of you familiar with the musical theater, please forgive me for defining the word 'book'. In a musical, the book is the libretto. The dialogue spoken, as opposed to the lyrics sung, constitute the so-called book. I told Childs that the last time I'd tried writing the book for a musical was in 1973, when

I'd teamed with Jerry Bock, the Pulitzer Prize composer of *Fiddler on the Roof*, on a mystery titled *Caper*! – which, by the way, was never produced. Childs seemed unfazed. In fact, he asked if I would take a look at a tape of the movie, and the book that had inspired it (he was now talking about the *novel* by Rowland Barber and not a *musical* 'book',) and the next morning both novel and tape arrived by Federal Express.

I found the movie unmemorable.

The novel, on the other hand, was fascinating. It did not call itself a novel, but surely that's what it was, even though real people propelled the complicated plot, even though the climax was apparently based on a night in 1925 when the real Legion of Decency raided and closed down the real Minsky's Burlesque. I called Childs at once, and told him I might be interested. We arranged to have lunch later that week.

Timothy Childs has to be about six-feet four-inches tall, a strikingly handsome man with snow white hair, a ruddy complexion, and a dazzling smile. Wearing a sports jacket and slacks, shirt unbuttoned at the throat, he strode into the restaurant he'd chosen on the West Side, extended his hand, told me at once that he agreed the movie was lousy, and then asked how I visualized the novel as a musical. I gave him some of the early ideas I'd been kicking around since reading it. I told him the novel was a gold mine, but that it was written in a convoluted style that would require much digging and rearranging to assemble into a dramatic whole. I told him that I saw doing it as a farce, with real-life action blending with actual burlesque skits to create a seamless whole. I told him that I was not a gag writer, although I had written several novels that could be termed 'comic'. I told him I'd written a play that folded on Broadway after three or four performances, but who was counting? I told him more about my experience with Jerry Bock and Stuart Ostrow, the producer who'd first approached me about doing a mystery musical. I told him I'd been actively involved in theater

LET'S TALK

during my college days, and that one of my sincere desires was to write the book for a musical comedy, which I considered the highest art form in America. I wasn't lying. I really believed this, and still believe it.

In turn, Tim – as I was already calling him – told me that Charles Strouse, the composer of *Annie* and *Applause* and *Bye Bye Birdie*, to name a few, was set to write the score for *Minsky's* (he also informed me that Strouse had written the score for the movie) and that the lyricist for the show was a man named Richard Maltby, Jr. who had co-written the lyrics for *Miss Saigon* and was currently represented on Broadway by the musical version of the movie *Big*. When he told me that Terrence McNally had already written a book that hadn't worked, I asked him how he'd happened to think of me as a replacement.

'Mike Ockrent is directing the show,' he said. 'He suggested you.'

My Round Robin tennis partner from Little Dix Bay!

The British director with whom my once-and-still-present wife did not wish to have dinner because there was nothing in it for her!

'And Susan Stroman will be choreographing,' Tim said. 'Do you think you might like to write it?'

Did I think I might like to write it?

I felt the way I had thirty-five years earlier, when Alfred Hitchcock called to ask if I'd like to write the screenplay for *The Birds*!

IN MAY OF 1996, WHEN the Charcoal Hill lease was about to expire, Evan and I began looking for another house to rent. We found an unfurnished cottage in Weston, a small grayish dwelling at the top of a hill, facing south and built so close to a river that it gave the impression of hanging over it. Surrounded by woods with blooming daffodils, nestled beneath big trees, unoccupied it looked abandoned and sad. The interior was small and simple. The front door opened directly onto a living room with a fireplace positioned so that it could serve the kitchen as well. The bedroom was small and long but with many windows, placed low. I noticed lily of the valley planted under the windows. There was only one old bathroom with just a shower, no tub. The kitchen was the only large room, renovated and fully equipped.

THE OWNER OF THE COTTAGE, in an act of unprecedented generosity, informed Dina and me that we could make any improvements we wanted, so long as we left them behind when our lease was up.

EVAN AND I KNEW THE place needed a lot of work, but it was irresistibly romantic. It was also very different from the sleek modern building we were considering as our base in New York.

'All we need is a place for the weekend,' we told ourselves. 'How beautiful it will be when we make some changes!' we kept saying.

Falling all over ourselves in finding reasons for taking the place.

WE HAD NO FURNITURE TO SPEAK OF.

On the first day of June, we moved in with only the stuff from Dina's apartment: her bed, her desk and the chair that went with it, two director's chairs, some bookcases and an answering machine. We moved the desk, its chair and the bookcases into a tiny room that served as my office. Our friends – Liz Fuller and her husband Reuel Dorman –

brought over a pair of lawn chairs which we coupled with an orange crate to form a living-room suite.

ALTHOUGH EVAN HAD STARTED DIVORCE proceedings immediately upon our return from what had been an unforgettable K-Club holiday, it was only now that I felt we were truly moving ahead. Those first several days in the cottage will always remain in my memory as a blissfully happy time in my life, when I was not only reassured of Evan's love but of his intentions as well. We were here, we were in love, we were happy and we were about to begin building our future together.

BUT THEN, GEE, WOULDN'T YOU know it?

On 9 June 1996, eight days after Dina and I moved into the cottage, I had my second heart attack.

EVAN KNEW EXACTLY WHAT WAS happening. His first heart attack had been seven years ago, but there wasn't any doubt that this was another one now.

IT WAS THE MIDDLE OF THE NIGHT.

Heart attacks – mine at least – always come in the middle of the night.

I knew the symptoms from the first time around the block. A terrible feeling of malaise. Something dreadful is about to happen. The first time, you can't imagine what it might be, you know only that you've never in your entire life felt this odd sense of impending disaster. The second time around, you know exactly what it is. The malaise is followed by a queasy feeling of vague nausea. And then the pain in your left shoulder starts, it moves down your arm, and you know this is it again, kiddies, this is it.

The ambulance couldn't find the entrance to the house.

Our landlady, because she thought it would improve real estate values, had listed the address as being on a road in *Westport* rather than Weston, where it was actually located. The ambulance driver spent twenty precious minutes trying to find us, until finally Dina called the hospital and once again gave directions.

I THINK I WAS STILL very calm right then.

I don't think I quite yet realized the danger Evan was in.

ON THE WAY TO NORWALK Hospital, Dina riding up front with the driver, me strapped to a stretcher in the back, with a black paramedic who kept patting my hand and telling me I'd be all right, I finally asked, 'Are we almost there?'

Like a kid to his father on a long road trip.

Are we almost there?

'Almost there,' he assured me.

'Because I think you're about to lose me,' I said.

'Nah, c'mon, man,' he said. 'Don't talk that way.'

THE TERROR CAME WHILE SITTING in the front seat of the ambulance watching Evan in pain. His cold sweat was gone now, and his skin was turning a pale blue. I remembered my father's color when he died of a heart attack at the age of fifty-six. He had turned a dark blue, and then almost purple and then he was suddenly pronounced dead.

I began to shake violently.

I looked at the driver, and then at the speedometer. There

was no traffic on the road. The ambulance lights engorged the center white line. I knew the driver was doing everything he could. Yet everything seemed a slow glide into the softness of the night. When I turned back to Evan, the technician was holding two paddles over his chest.

AT THE ENTRANCE TO THE hospital's emergency room, they rushed me out of the ambulance on a stretcher.

It had begun to drizzle.

I scrunched up my face against the light rain.

A nurse remarked, 'Oooo, he doesn't like that.'

I WAS TOLD THAT EVAN was out of immediate danger just now but we wouldn't know how much damage had been done to the heart until tests were done in the morning. For now, he would be moved into the Intensive Care Unit. I pleaded to see him and was almost surprised at the ease with which the request was granted.

He lay in bed, attached to many instruments. His face was very pale, as if – drained of the blue – there was no color left at all. He was exhausted and looked vulnerable. But he knew that I was in the room and he managed a weak smile. His lips moved to form the words 'I love you,' and I crossed my arms over my chest in the familiar gesture we used on the street when we were too far from each other to hear the words.

He's safe, I thought.

We're going to make it.

ON 20 JUNE 1996, AT St. Vincent's Hospital in Bridgeport, they performed my second angioplasty in seven years.

(I would later joke that I had heart attacks every seven years and divorces every twenty-two years.)

I know I've mentioned this procedure before but perhaps I should explain it again more fully. An angioplasty is an invasive procedure performed to reduce or eliminate blockages in coronary arteries, thereby restoring the flow of blood to blood-deprived heart tissue. Opening a blockage – also called a 'plaque' – in a coronary artery involves the use of an angioplasty balloon.

This balloon is a tiny little thing which, when deflated, slides easily into a guide wire that is passed through a needle puncture made in the groin's femoral artery. As the guide wire is threaded up the artery toward the heart, the doctors watch its progress on a small screen. When the wire reaches the blockage, they inflate the balloon, and it flattens the plaque against the walls of the artery. Because the doctors must give constant instruction – 'Take a deep breath . . . hold it . . . let it out . . . breathe normally' – the patient is awake throughout the entire painless procedure.

The first time I had an angioplasty, the doctors were talking about a movie they'd seen. This time they were discussing the pros and cons of something new in cardiology, a 'stent' that could be implanted after angioplasty to keep the artery open and prevent the regrowth of plaque.

I wanted to say, 'Hey, pay attention here!'

But they were inside my heart.

IT WAS A LONG, SLOW RECOVERY.

I felt weak, I felt depressed, I felt vulnerable, I felt like an invalid, and I frankly wondered if I would ever be able to get back to the computer full-time again.

It was not until 30 August that I felt strong enough to take any sort of trip. Dina and I left for Italy, and did not return to Connecticut until the twentieth of September.

Two weeks later, in Baltimore, I had another heart attack.

THE EVENING BEFORE, I HAD signed books for Paige Rose at her *Mystery Loves Company* store in Baltimore. Dina and I were scheduled to leave for home this Saturday morning, but I'd awakened with a slight feeling of queasiness that was all too reminiscent of a familiar sense of malaise. There was no excruciating pain – but neither had there been the first or second times around. Johns Hopkins Hospital was only several blocks away from our hotel. It was a bright, sunny October morning; I suggested to Dina that we walk over there, 'Just to make sure, okay, honey?'

The emergency room doctors examined me and told me they thought a heart attack was 'evolving'. They felt the angioplasty performed in June was failing, and that the artery was now closing in again. They suggested that another angioplasty be done in order to save the lower part of my heart. When I asked them when we should do this, they answered, 'Now, at once, immediately, as soon as an OR is free.'

THE THING ABOUT MEDICAL EMERGENCIES is that your life is entirely in the hands of Medland strangers. I did not know the cardiologists who performed the angioplasty in Baltimore, I could not under torture tell you their names now. But they were inside my heart again, casually discussing the weather or last night's great shore dinner while they inflated their little balloon and opened my artery again.

They did a good job. I didn't die.

Only part of my heart did.

In truth, this was an enormous relief.

If the damn thing was finally dead, I couldn't have any more heart attacks.

I got back to work full time the very next week.

AFTER OUR FIRST MEETING TOGETHER on *Minsky's*, Richard Maltby told us quite honestly that he didn't think he could write the lyrics for the kind of show we had in mind. Timothy Childs brought in Susan Birkenhead as the new lyricist. Susan had written the lyrics for *Jelly's Last Jam*, and had worked before with such musical giants as Jule Styne and Luther Henderson.

To my knowledge, Charles Strouse had never collaborated with a woman lyricist before, and I was afraid at first that the relationship might prove to be an uneasy one. But they certainly seemed to be working as a team when – a week or so after I delivered an outline for the book – the three of us met in Mike Ockrent's new offices at Warner Brothers on Fifty-third Street. Warner's had recently signed him to a production deal, and Mike was inordinately proud of his new digs, showing us around, introducing us to his secretary, bristling over the fact that his name on the lobby directory was MICHAEL OCKRENT, and not the MIKE OCKRENT for which he was deservedly famous.

For the past several months, I'd been digging through the truly convoluted Rowland Barber novel in search of golden nuggets, and had finally devised an outline that mixed burlesque skits with a rising dramatic line (I hoped) that led inexorably to the night of the infamous Legion of Decency raid, indicating at the same time every occasion where I thought a song would serve better than dialogue. I was feeling very good about what I'd written.

We sat together around a long table in the conference room, and Mike asked Susan and Charles if they'd read the outline, and they both acknowledged that they had. He told me I'd done some very good work, and marveled at the wealth of material I'd found in the book, asked which of the skits were original and which were actually from burlesque, and then said, 'But *suppose* . . .'

And went on to outline an entirely new approach to the show!

I listened in total amazement as he politely ignored everything I'd written, and proposed instead the story of an English girl who comes to New York in search of an American with whom she'd had a brief love affair in London, somehow finding her way into Minsky's Burlesque, where she becomes the subject of a bet about taking off her clothes.

Susan and Charles sat at the table, smiling, nodding.

You have to understand that whereas I was relatively new to the theater, I had been around the Hollywood block once or twice, and was not exactly new to collaboration. I realized, too, that the book writer was low man on the totem pole in the world of musical comedy, and I knew I was dealing here with experienced people who knew far more than I did about musicals. Once upon a time, I'd written the screenplay for a science-fiction film titled *Saturn Three*, and after I delivered it, the director – who happened to be Stanley Donen – called to say (and I quote), 'This is the worst screenplay I've ever read.' Aghast, I simply answered, 'Well, that's the first time I've ever heard *that*!'

Now, sitting across the table from a still-smiling director, who – like Donen before him – had virtually told me he was discarding everything I'd come up with, I could only say, 'Well, your approach is nothing like the movie *or* the novel.'

'Can you make it work?' Mike asked.

'I can try,' I said.

Tightly.

THE DOORBELL TO OUR LITTLE cottage rang at six in the morning. The sun was still not up. This was the second day of February, 1997, a cold dark Sunday morning. In four days, Dina and I would be leaving for Southeast Asia. I had contracted to write an article for an online magazine called *Mungo*. They were paying all my expenses, plus a hefty writing fee, and Abercrombie and Kent – the travel company arranging the trip – was giving us a break on Dina's air fare and expenses. We were still in bed when the doorbell rang. Dina put on a robe, and went to the door to answer it.

'Who is it?' I called from the other end of the cottage.

'Miss Bee-mee-tridge-evv-ee-uh?' a man's voice asked.

Close, but no cigar. In fact, not even close.

By then, I was out of bed and into my own robe. The man standing just outside our living-room door was wearing a sheriff's uniform. He mangled Dina's name once again, and when she confirmed that she was indeed Miss *Dimitrijevic*, he handed her a subpoena with the name 'Ms. Dragica Bemitrijevia' on it.

The subpoena read:

By the Authority of the State of Connecticut, you are hereby commanded to appear at Schoonmaker & George, P.C., 5 Edgewood Ave. Greenwich, on February 4, 1997 at 10:00 A.M. to testify what you know in a certain civil action pending between Evan Hunter, Plaintiff and Mary Vann Hunter, Defendant . . .

Schoonmaker & George were my wife's Connecticut attorneys, associates of her New York bomber, who should have at least told them how to spell Dina's last name. February 4 was exactly two days from now, and exactly two days before we were scheduled to leave on our trip.

But that wasn't the half of it.

The subpoena went on to say:

AND you are further commanded to bring with you

and produce at that time and place SEE SCHEDULE
A ATTACHED HERETO.

Schedule A read:

Your Green card.

Copies of federal and state income tax returns for
the past three years (individual and/or joint)
including all attached schedules, W-2 forms and
1099 forms.

All marriage certificates and divorce papers from
any previous marriages.

Copies of any and all tickets for travel during the
past two years and any such tickets for future
travel.

Any and all bank statements for checking or
savings accounts in your name, either
individually or jointly, for the past five years.

Copies of any and all diplomas in your name from
a college or university.

Copy of your driver's license.

Copies of all credit card bills and/or statements in
your name for the past two years.

Copies of any and all employment contracts with
theaters involving your work.

Copies of any news clippings, from the United
States or abroad, about your work in the
theater.

Any and all letters from Evan Hunter from the
time of January 1, 1995 to the present.

Copy of your passport.

Any and all contracts with New York University
for a position as an acting teacher.

Copies of any and all employment agreements
between yourself and any employer for the past
five years.

Wow!

At six in the morning, no less!

To me, this appeared to be simple harassment, an attempt to besmirch Dina's good name or to belittle her credibility. An attempt to cast her in the role of The Other Woman. The Bimbo.

My attorneys saw it in a different light.

They interpreted it as a transparent effort to get her deported.

IT WAS THOUGHT PRUDENT TO hire a lawyer other than my own to represent Dina. He worked for us all the while we were in Southeast Asia, and on 14 April 1997, we received the following letter:

> I am pleased to tell you that Judge Harrigan granted in full the relief sought in our Motion to Quash subpoena. He stated that although Ms. Dimitrijevic is required to appear at any deposition, she is not required to bring one piece of paper with her. He indicated that we would be justified in making objections to matters that are not relevant to the divorce litigation.

That very same day, I finished the 94-page first-draft script for *The Night They Raided Minsky's*, and Fed Exxed copies of it to Tim, Mike, Susan and Charles. Five days later, Dina and I left for Italy again, where I taught a whirlwind course in writing at the Holden School in Torino. On April 26, we were back home again, and three days after that, I resumed work on *The Last Best Hope*. I still hadn't finished the novel when Dina and I left for Oslo on 5 June to accept a crime writers' prize there. My work calendar shows that there'd been two *Minsky* meetings in New York before we left for Norway.

I did not get back to the show full time until 15 July. At the beginning of August, Ghossein wrote the following letter to Blaugrund:

Dear Stanley:

I saw Mr. Hunter today who is now two years after completion of external radiotherapy for hyperplasia and parakeratosis of the right vocal cord.

He has no significant hoarseness and is asymptomatic. I do not detect any cervical adenopathy. On indirect laryngoscopy there is no suspicious finding noted. Both cords are mobile with no significant post-radiation sequelae. The remaining part of the head and neck examination is negative. I understand that you are following him regularly and therefore I gave him a follow-up appointment for one year.

Sincerely yours,

N.A. Ghossein, M.D.

By the end of August, I had delivered another draft of the *Minsky's* script and almost finished the Matthew Hope novel.

I had also finally got my divorce.

Finally!

En fin!

Finalmente!

We left for Milan on 4 September. On 7 September, an interview with me appeared in *Corriere Della Sera*, Italy's largest newspaper. This was its first paragraph:

Il celebrato scrittore di polizieschi sembra cadere in un roseo incantamento mentre osserva rapito la futura terza moglie, Dragica Dimitrijevic, una ragazza slava di aggraziata eleganza.

Lei ricambia con commossa tenerezza definendo il futuro secondo marito 'artefice di ogni magia'.

Loosely translated, it read:

The celebrated writer of police procedurals seems to be falling into a rosy-tinted enchantment right now, while he looks in awe at his future third wife, Dragica Dimitrijevic, a Yugoslavian girl of graceful elegance. She does the same, moved and tender, while she defines her future second husband as 'the creator of every magic'.

FOR THE LOCATION OF OUR wedding, Evan and I considered anywhere in the entire world. But we could not find a better place for us to get married than the gardens of the Hotel Cipriani in Venice. The date we chose was September ninth, 9/9, divine numbers in Chinese numerology and in my belief.

The civil ceremony took place in New York City, on September fourth, and it was possible only thanks to our friend, Kathleen Landis. I knew my beautiful friend almost as long as I'd lived in New York. I first met her as my piano teacher. She played piano (and still does) in the lounge at the Hotel Pierre, where I would often stop by for an after-theater drink. She helped me navigate the social scene in New York, to which I was a perfect stranger, and when Evan and I met, she helped me organize a surprise birthday party for him at the Pierre. They took an instant liking to each other.

So, when we were told that we could not have a civil wedding without a necessary delay from the day a license was issued, which would ruin our carefully planned trip to Venice and the wedding there, I enlisted my friend's help once again. What came next was the happiest coincidence we could hope for. Kathleen knew a judge who was a great admirer of Evan Hunter/Ed McBain. The very next day, still putting together my bridal bouquet, I was in a taxi with my husband-to-be, and Kathleen, and Howard Lucas (her significant other for almost all her adult life, and a wonderful pianist in his own right). Evan and I were married in the privacy of the judge's office, by the judge himself. After the ceremony, Jane Gelfman, Evan's agent, surprised us with champagne. We all raised a toast. Evan and I were officially husband and wife.

In the picture that Kathleen gave me later, the man wearing a dark blue suit and the woman wearing a blue dress and holding a small bouquet of yellow, white and pink roses are lost in their first embrace as husband and wife. This picture captures completely the memory I hold of the actual occasion. But the full realization of the love Evan and I shared then, and still share, came to me only later, on our honeymoon in Portofino. It was then that I knew my life had changed forever, and I would no longer be the lonely, often sad woman I'd been before.

EVAN IS A LAPSED CATHOLIC, and completely indifferent to religious ceremonies. I was born Greek Orthodox, but I believe that there is one God who will welcome me equally into a temple in Bali, or a cathedral in Rome, or my own small Orthodox church in Glavica. For our wedding, I wanted a priest who could embrace my own beliefs while uniting Evan and me in love and mutual respect for each other.

I knew of such a man.

I had first met Branislav Lecic ten years earlier. He was performing on a stage in Dubrovnik, under an open sky, playing a man condemned to a dungeon and surrounded by stone walls. As the audience watched breathlessly, certain he would fall to his death, he climbed those walls stone by stone, his hands reaching for the stars. I went backstage later to talk to him, and we became instant good friends. The immediate bond forged between us was of a kind that will never let us feel separate from each other. True soul-brother and -sister, we don't need to talk often, but we are always present in each other's lives. Today, Branislav is the Serbian Minister of Culture. When I called him in Belgrade, he was merely (merely!) a prominent actor and movie star – but he also happened to be an ordained priest. I told him that Evan and I would be getting married in Venice, and he said at once, 'I'm a priest. I will marry you.'

He was due to arrive in Venice with his gorgeous wife, Ivana, on the night before our wedding. But the skies had opened in a terrible storm, and a torrent of rain was falling upon the city, cutting off electricity everywhere. In a small restaurant on a side street, Evan and I dined alone by candle-light, wondering how we could possibly be married the next day, wondering how (or even *if*) our priest would ever arrive. Later that night, when the storm had subsided, and the four of us sat sipping cappuccino on the Piazza San Marco, Branislav told us, 'It was almost a medieval experience, approaching Venice in the dark, from a raging sea!' The contact between him and Evan was effortless and instant. It was as if they'd known each other for centuries, and were simply catching up and filling in. At the end of the evening, as we were parting, Branislav said, in Serbo-Croatian, '*Naš čovek.*' I translated this for Evan. What Branislav had truly meant was: 'Your man has no boundaries. He is not only the country he represents, he embraces your heritage as well, the values you are bringing; he and you are becoming one.'

The next day was going to be my wedding day.

THE MORNING OF OUR WEDDING, Evan went down to the hotel barber to have his hair and his beard trimmed. When he came back up to the room, I took one look at him and said, 'We're not getting married!'

His mustaches were crooked, his beard had patches in it as if he'd suddenly contracted some terrible skin disease, and the hair on his head was cut so short that a visible white line just below the hairline gave him the appearance of a man whose scalp was not fully attached to his face.

We decided to shave the beard off completely, but this only added to the disaster. The beard of two years, now freshly shaved, left what seemed to be oversensitive skin underneath, turning redder by the minute, and all our efforts to calm it with lotion only brought out more blotches. We were both miserable.

And I still had to have *my* hair done!

At the same hotel barber shop!

Uneasily, braid in hand, I explained that I wanted my long hair to be left loose except for the hairpiece, which I wanted to wear braided on top of my head to support a crown made of small white pearls. I told the stylist I was looking for a romantic, medieval look.

This was not meant to be.

Instead she teased my hair so that it stood out all over my head, like the coiffe of a sixties beauty queen! I could not face my future husband with yet this new disaster. In the ladies' room of the hotel lobby, I combed out my hair, letting it hang loose again to my shoulders, the way I wear it every day. Back in the room, I attached the crown with hairpins and hid them with flowers I took from my wedding bouquet. Simple. And very much me, I thought. But my heart was pounding.

EVAN AND I WALKED HAND in hand along a flowering path to where Branislav, our priest, was waiting for us. It was a gorgeous day, without even a trace of last night's storm, the sky a bright blue, the rays of the morning sun reflecting on the leaves in the canopy above our heads. The plants lining our way were so dense that I felt we were walking along a secret path. Walking in step with Evan, I held tight to his hand, wondering if he was as happy as I was. Did I only imagine butterflies landing on flowers everywhere around us, birds chirping in the trees as we followed the path to where Branislav, dressed in his priestly robes, was waiting for us, a Bible in his hands? Standing beside him was Ivana, all in white, two tall, large, white candles in her hands. She lit both candles and handed one to each of us, to hold and to keep the flames alive, as they represented our souls. Purifying the path with burning incense, Branislav led us toward an altar set between two large urns filled with flowers. Before this altar was a small stage covered with a red carpet, a red cushion on it. Evan and I passed the garden space on our left, walled by evergreens and flowering vines, where tables were set for our reception. Beyond, I could see boats passing by on the canal. Our guests were seated slightly to the right of the altar, a colorful blur of green, yellow and pink, some ladies wearing large hats, but I was too afraid to take my eyes off the candles to look closer. Watching the burning wicks, both of us carefully shielding them with cupped hands, Evan and I approached the altar.

The ceremony was in Serbo-Croatian. Evan later joked that he hadn't understood a word of it and didn't know what he was getting into. Actually, as Branislav spoke the solemn words, Ivana translated them for Evan and our friends. In keeping with custom and tradition, Branislav bound our wrists together with a white silk scarf. We knelt before him on the red cushion, and he tilted the candles so that both flames were joined in a single, brighter flame. We exchanged our vows, and he freed our hands again. There were tears in Evan's eyes as he placed the ring on my finger, smiling. We kissed, and a cheer went up from our friends. Happy and tearful, we all started toward the festive tables, where

Bellinis, and champagne, and wonderful food, and a magnificent wedding cake decorated with miniature gondolas awaited us.

That evening we carried champagne with us to where real gondolas were waiting to take all the wedding guests out onto the moonlit canals. I had changed from my long, satin, white dress into a red chiffon, and I was carrying a single red rose with me. We ended the evening with dinner at a small restaurant on a small piazza.

The next morning, we left for our honeymoon in Portofino.

AN ALLEY LINED WITH CAMELLIAS led us to a small terrace chiseled into the cliff above a pool nestled at the foot of the hotel, embraced on both sides by gardens. The view from the terrace took our breaths away. A vast horizon descended to the port in the distance, its stillness disturbed only by occasional flocks of birds. Colorful houses spread behind dark blue waters bobbing with anchored boats.

We made ourselves comfortable in lounge chairs on the terrace, an open umbrella between them. I placed the bottles of nail polish – red, and white, and black – on a small table under the umbrella. Then I began painting the big toenails on my husband's feet.

I painted a man's smiling face on his left big toenail.

I painted a woman's smiling face on his right big toenail.

White faces, big red smiling mouths, black eyebrows and eyes, black button noses.

We drifted off in the sun, a stillness on the air. From the corner of my eye, I saw a baby lizard making his way up the vines caught between the cracks of the stone. He began moving toward us, his tiny shadow, sharp in the morning sun, following him over the stoned terrace. He stopped at the foot of Evan's chair. His body lifted, tummy exposed. He fixed his eyes on me. Behind him and above him were my husband's big toes with their painted faces of a man and a woman smiling happily. The lizard seemed to be smiling, too.

And then . . .

It was as if the force of love suddenly turned a bright golden spot on me, touching me softly, filling my senses with potent joy. All at once, I felt completely at home, living the married bliss the ancient fables only told of. I had reached at last a place the universe had reserved for me, and I could see with clarity the woman I'd become, beloved and in love, stronger than ever to defend the riches the gods had bestowed upon me.

Happiness.

I was a happily married woman.

IN THE WEEKS AND MONTHS that followed my wedding to Dina, I cannot tell you how many times I sat at the dining-room table in the Ockrent apartment on West 57th Street, reading *Minsky's* for potential investors. The two leading roles were Billy Minsky, and the British girl Mike had invented. I would read Billy, Stro would read Whatever Her Name Was – she was soon to become history – and Charles, Susan, and Mike himself would read all the other characters. Our arranger, Glen Kelly (I called him 'Glenkelly, Glenross') sat at the piano and played the score. Stro and Susan Birkenhead sang all the female parts, Charles and Mike sang the supporting male roles. I joined in whenever there was a full chorus number, but I did not sing any of Billy's songs. These were sung by Glen at the piano. This had nothing to do with the sonority or volume of my voice. Ever since the radiation treatments, I could yell (or sing) as loud as anyone in New York. It just had to do with the fact that I was a lousy singer.

Once, after I sang with the chorus at one of these backer's

auditions, Mike took me aside and said, 'Maybe you shouldn't sing quite so loudly, Evan.'

I said, 'Is that a director's clever way of telling me I can't sing?'

Mike rolled his eyes heavenward and held up his hands in total innocence.

'Why, you have a positively *beautiful* voice!' he said, and we both burst out laughing.

Our relationship had not always been so convivial.

I remember going to the 57th Street apartment in time for breakfast one morning . . .

I had bought a house in Connecticut shortly after the final divorce papers were signed and Dina and I were now splitting our time between our new home in Weston and an apartment we were renting on East 72nd Street. She had enrolled in NYU's film school, and was attending classes every weekday. I would drive down to NYU to pick her up after school every Friday, and we'd drive back to the country together, and then come in again on Sunday night to begin the next day's classes and *Minsky* meetings all over again.

Anyway, that morning I got to the apartment earlier than either Susan or Charles, and while Mike and I were having coffee and bagels together in the kitchen, I said, 'Mike, there's something we have to discuss.'

He looked at me.

Thought I was kidding at first.

We kidded a lot. This was, after all, a show about burlesque. Lots of jokes. Lots of kidding around.

I said, 'Mike, you dismiss everything I do. I write a scene, and you say, "But *suppose* . . ." and then you give me your take on it, which is entirely different from mine, and . . . no, let me finish, please.'

He held up his hands.

Okay. Talk.

'In effect, you're not giving me a chance, Mike. You're

throwing away everything I write. I think I have something to contribute here, and I'd like the chance to do it. If you want me to phone it in instead, just tell me, and I'll phone it in. If that's what you want, fine. I'd rather you listened to me, though, I'd rather you gave my work a chance.'

He looked at me.

He nodded.

'Okay,' he said.

'Okay?'

'Point taken,' he said.

We shook hands.

MY WORK CALENDARS SHOW THAT in the first three months of 1998, I spent forty-six days on *Minsky's*. By the beginning of April, we were ready to go into rehearsal for our first full-cast reading. We'd been auditioning Equity actors all day long, and had finally chosen our Billy and the lovelorn British girl. At six that evening, Mike sat us all down at a long table, and said, 'I won't be directing the reading.'

We thought he was joking at first.

Another joke, right?

The show was full of jokes.

'Stro will be taking over for now,' he said.

Someone asked why. Maybe it was me. I'm not sure now.

'I have to go into the hospital,' Mike said. 'I have leukemia.'

MIKE WAS LOSING HIS HAIR and was wearing a baseball cap. Charles and Stro *always* wore baseball caps. It looked like a meeting of the New York Yankees; only Susan and I were hatless. We were there to discuss the recent reading.

I told everyone that I felt the show had serious problems. I told them I didn't believe the cockamamie British girl for a moment, and I didn't believe the bet that forced her to take off her clothes, and I didn't believe her falling in love with Billy. I told them we could make some minor changes and go ahead with essentially what we had, but that wouldn't win us any Tonys.

'Besides,' I said, 'I don't want a Tony. I want the Pulitzer.'

Mike listened.

He always listened to me now. After our Kitchen Summit Meeting, we had become true collaborators. In fact, he had asked if I would agree to a 'Conceived by Evan Hunter and Mike Ockrent' credit, and I had told him I would.

We spent all morning and part of the afternoon kicking it around. And then I made what was probably my first valuable contribution to the show.

We were discussing who should replace the British girl as our lead.

I was silent for a long time.

'Yes?' Mike said.

I looked up.

'Something?' he said.

'I think I know who she should be,' I said.

'Who?'

'Someone who works for the Legion of Decency.'

'Of *course*!' Mike said at once.

It was perfect.

Billy Minsky falling in love with the woman who was trying to put him out of business! We were on our way again.

WHEN I DELIVERED THE NEXT draft of the script, Mike called to tell me how marvelous he thought it was. 'A real breakthrough,' he said, 'truly marvelous, Evan.' Shortly thereafter, The Ahmanson Theater in Los Angeles agreed to do the show in the summer of 2000, for a two-month run prior to a Broadway opening. Everything in my life now seemed to be moving along beautifully. I had a show coming to Broadway!

I had delivered two new 87th Precinct novels and was working on a new Evan Hunter novel. And I was now married to a woman who thought I was ... well ... wonderful. What a grand feeling to wake up in the morning and feel ... well ... loved.

In September of 1999, Dina and I sent out invitations that were headlined **9/9/99**. It was our second wedding anniversary. I wrote a little skit for Dina and me to perform for our guests, and while she and I were rehearsing it, she cautioned in her gentle, accented voice, 'Honey, there can only be one director, you know.'

My other director, Mike Ockrent, didn't laugh very much when we performed the script. Stro was in rehearsal with *Contact*, the show that would later win her a Tony award for Best Musical, and he was there alone that night, so I thought his despondency was due to her absence. But when I asked him why he seemed so exceedingly glum, he told me that after a lengthy remission, his cancer was back, and he'd been forced to postpone a bone marrow transplant yet another time.

On December 2, Mike died.

He was fifty-three years old.

A MONTH OR SO EARLIER, we'd had a long serious talk about mortality. We were on the telephone – most of our conversations in those last days were on the telephone – and he wondered aloud how this could possibly be happening to him. This wasn't something he had brought upon himself, this wasn't the result of too much smoking or drinking or eating things that were bad for you, this was just something that had come out of the blue.

He told me the doctors had no idea what had caused it. There was even speculation that it came from gamma rays in outer space. He told me he'd been doing a lot of thinking about the work he'd done and the work he still hoped to do. He told me they would be doing the transplant soon, and I said, 'That's good news,' and he said, 'Well, not really. They say only one in four is successful,' and I said, 'Those are good odds, Mike,' but we both knew they were not good odds. And yet, to the very end, we were all certain that this thing would not take Mike from us. This thing could not take someone who was brimming with life every minute of the day. It could not. It would not *dare*.

But it had.

BY APRIL OF THE YEAR 2000, I had finished a novel titled *Candyland*, the first half of which was written by Evan Hunter, the second half by Ed McBain – talk about schizophrenia! But this was more than a stunt. Instead, it was an attempt to demonstrate the essential differences between a writer who thought of himself as 'literary' (you should pardon the expression) and a writer who wrote mere 'entertainments' (thank you, Graham Greene). The styles in each half of the book were enormously different, as was the approach to the subject matter. Once a reader started the second half, he knew instantly that he was on McBain turf. There was no doubt in my mind that this would explain it once and for all time.

The next month, I began work immediately on an 87th Precinct mystery titled *Money, Money, Money*. Without any *Minsky* distractions – after Mike's death, the Ahmanson engagement had been postponed indefinitely, and everything was on hold – I finished 226 pages of the book before Dina and I left for a month-long vacation in the south of France.

On the plane over, we both caught colds.

When we returned home on 26 August, my throat was still hoarse.

From the cold, I figured.

MINSKY'S WAS COMING ALIVE AGAIN!

In my absence, Tim Childs had turned over the production reins to a hugely successful company called Scorpio Entertainment, Inc., and another Equity reading was planned for October. That same month, Dina and I left for Frankfurt where I won the $10,000 prize for best fiction for my novel *The Last Dance*, which had been released as an e-book shortly after its hardcover publication. We got home on 21 October, and cast and rehearsed *Minsky's* for the next four days. This time Charles Strouse directed the reading. Once again the Ahmanson people were there. And once again, they loved it, and plans were made for an opening the following fall. By December, Jerry Zaks – who had recently directed the enormously successful revival of *Something Funny Happened on the Way to the Forum* – agreed to direct *Minsky's*. I had by then finished and delivered the new 8-7, and *Candyland* had just been published to rave reviews that seemed to understand the differences between my two personae. I was beginning to smell the roses again.

Then – late in December, just before I was about to start the *Candyland* book tour – a routine CAT scan suggested by my urologist revealed an aneurysm of the abdominal aorta.

THE AORTA IS THE MAJOR artery that carries blood from the heart to the rest of the body. The abdominal aorta supplies blood to the liver, the spleen, the intestines and the kidneys. Lower down, the abdominal aorta divides into two arteries that supply blood to the legs.

An aneurysm is a bulging or ballooning of an artery wall. Think of it as a blister on an inner tube.

If an aneurysm bursts, you are usually dead before you can get to a hospital.

Jonathan Larson, the thirty-five-year-old composer of the hit musical, *Rent*, had died from an undiagnosed aortic aneurysm the night before the show made its off-Broadway debut.

I was supposed to leave for San Francisco on 3 January to begin a seven-city *Candyland* tour that would end in Bryn Mawr, Pennsylvania on the thirteenth.

When I asked my doctor if I could postpone an operation until the tour was over, he looked at me as if I were totally nuts.

Fifteen thousand Americans die every year from ruptures of abdominal aortic aneurysms. It is the tenth leading cause of death in males over fifty-five years of age. Another factor contributing to an AAA – as it is known in the trade – is smoking. I had smoked two packs of cigarettes a day until my first heart attack in 1989. I was undoubtedly male. And I had just turned seventy-four in October.

This was beginning to get comical.

I was beginning to feel like the Bionic Man.

ON 17 JANUARY, THREE DAYS after *Candyland* appeared on the Los Angeles Times bestseller list, Dina and I flew out to the Cleveland Clinic. On a bleak Friday morning, two days later, Triple-A surgery was performed to repair the life-threatening balloon in my aorta.

The operation was a long and difficult one.

In order to repair an aneurysm, the diseased area of the aorta is entirely removed and replaced with an artificial Dacron graft, which is then sewn into place. But the aorta is buried deep inside the body, close to the spine, and in order to get to it, a lot of organs must be moved aside. I don't imagine my liver or my intestines were lying there exposed on the operating table, but certainly a great deal of cautious and careful manipulation was necessary – and this took a great deal of time and patience.

Six and a half hours, to be exact.

Recovery took a lot longer.

I LEFT THE HOSPITAL ON 27 January, and did not write anything again until 12 February. I have to explain that sixteen days away from the computer is quite unusual for me. I was trained to believe that if I don't write something today, there'll be no check in the mail six months from today. Normally, I try to write at least eight pages a day, and I feel guilty if I don't reach that goal. But, at last, on the twelfth day of February, I was writing again!

What I wrote was a three-line haiku.

I beg your pardon?

A haiku is a Japanese verse form consisting of three unrhymed lines of five, seven and five syllables respectively, for a total of seventeen syllables. Most haiku contain a seasonal reference. I knew nothing about any of this until a dear friend of mine named Akira Naoi suggested that I write one. Akira has written perhaps the most definitive reference books on the 87th Precinct. Whenever I need to find out which cop got shot in which book, I e-mail Akira. In 2001, he was still living in the Stone Age, and so we corresponded by airmail. It was he who told me that a haiku in English was better with thirteen syllables than with seventeen. The poem I sent him on 12 February contained exactly thirteen syllables. It read:

> *This winter, I mend*
> *Day by day, bit by bit,*
> *Slowly.*

On 14 March, a bit more than a month later, I sent him another haiku with thirteen syllables in it:

> *I eat. I laugh.*
> *I spring forward*
> *Into the sunlight*

Please note how cleverly I sneaked the season into the second line. Please note, too, that I was writing again. Even if my poems weren't all that good, twenty-six syllables in a month wasn't all that bad.

Moreover, the hoarseness in my throat, which had been lingering ever since we'd come back from France, had disappeared entirely. Miracle of miracles! Repairing the aneurysm seemed to have cured my cold as well!

The other miracle was that Dina was still with me.

FROM ALMOST THE MOMENT WE'D met, I'd brought this wonderful woman nothing but grief. A heart attack in June of 1996, another one that October when the angioplasty failed in Baltimore, a bitter divorce battle that had filled more than two years of our lives with so much stress and anger that I was truly surprised I hadn't already died of a stroke! And now the aneurysm.

Dina had lived through all this.

But she was still here.

And she was there with me again, on 17 March, when we went to see Dr. Slavit yet another time.

There are no miracles, there is no magic.

The hoarseness cured by my Triple-A surgery had returned.

*

WHAT?

What!

Oh yes. After examining me, Slavit determined that all those various tubes inserted into my throat during the surgery in Cleveland had caused a swelling, which in turn had caused the vocal cords to close properly – but only temporarily. Now that the swelling had subsided, the cords no longer touched, and the weakness and the hoarseness of voice had returned.

Bummer.

Slavit found no apparent lesions, no nodules or polyps. He suggested, however, that an injection of either collagen or fat into the left vocal cord might give it the bulk necessary for 'proper closure and subsequent improvement of voice quality'.

On 22 March, I wrote a letter to Dr. Floyd D. Loop, CEO of the Cleveland Clinic Foundation. It read in part:

Dear Dr. Loop:

Please forgive me for not answering your gracious letter sooner but recovery has been a sort of up and down process here. One day I'm depressed and weeping, the next I'm at the computer typing away. Things get better and better all the time, however. Tomorrow will mark nine weeks since the surgery. And I feel I'm finally on the way to full recovery.

That same week, I went back to work part-time, stitching together four of my short stories as a screenplay for a possible movie. It must have been an unusually long winter in Connecticut because there was still snow on the ground on 5 May, when I sent Akira my next poem. *Fourteen* syllables this time. I was getting stronger.

Snow glistening white
Footprints leading
Only to the sun

ON 22 MAY, I WENT into Lenox Hill yet again, this time to have fat 'harvested' from my abdomen and injected into the left vocal cord. I tolerated the procedure well, and left the hospital that very same day.

On 30 May, Slavit sent me to an allergist to determine whether or not allergies might be contributing to my voice problems. It was discovered that I was allergic to dust, dust mites, and molds, and it was recommended that I avoid substances producing these allergies.

On 6 June, Susan, Charles and I received a letter from Messrs. Baruch, Viertel, Frankel and Routh of Scorpio Entertainment, Inc. It told us they were moving to the sidelines on the MINSKY project.

That same month Ken Mandelbaum wrote in his column for *The Insider*:

Meanwhile, the future of the musical, *The Night They Raided Minsky's*, appears to be a question mark. The show had a Jerry Zaks-directed reading last month, with Reg Rogers and Erin Dilly in the leading roles. It had been mentioned to play L.A.'s Ahmanson in autumn 2002 (the second time it was scheduled to play there; *The Dead* replaced it last year), with Broadway the obvious goal. But I'm hearing that *Minsky's* may not be going forward, with one theory suggesting that the show's feel might be too similar to *The Producers*.

The roses were beginning to wither.
In fact, they were getting ready to die.

*

MY HAIKU SEEMED TO REFLECT a growing melancholy.

On the Fourth of July that year, I wrote and airmailed to Akira:

> *Swiftly falling rain*
> *Going, going, gone.*
> *It is summer now.*

On 15 July, I wrote:

> *Summer lightning.*
> *Birds take wing.*
> *I, too, am afraid.*

And on the first of August, this went off to Japan:

> *I have seen the seasons*
> *Come and go, all four.*
> *There must be more.*

> *And that same day:*

> *September seems so near*
> *The leaves already rattle.*
> *Merry Christmas.*

Seventeen syllables. Exactly like the Japanese.

The year 2002 was just around the corner.

I WAS NOT BEING NEGLIGENT, I swear to you.

Neither were my doctors.

If anything, we were overly cautious and diligent.

Between 22 May 2001 – when they harvested that fat from around my belly button and injected it into my left vocal cord – to 16 July 2002, more than a year later, I visited Slavit a total of thirteen times. Virtually once a month. During those visits, he examined and re-examined a developing bump on the left cord where the needle had been inserted for the fat injection; he examined and re-examined a large polyp-like swelling on the left cord; he remarked upon the worsening of my voice, and he planned removal of the polyp. But nothing seemed too terribly urgent. Business as usual. No cancer.

And life went on.

In October, Slavit surgically removed the polyp from my left vocal cord.

Pathology did not reveal cancer cells.

My voice seemed better after the surgery, and there was better closure of the vocal cords, even if the left cord was still a little stiff.

During my November visit to Slavit's office – this was still 2001, a full seven months before that fateful day of 16 July 2002 – he found no lesions on the vocal cords. None. Not on the right cord, not on the left. Nothing. Nada. Zilch.

In December, there were still no lesions, and my voice was a little better. It was not until March of 2002 that a small web at the V-joining of the cords presented itself, and not until June – after my voice had been exceedingly hoarse for a full month – that yet another polyp appeared. Slavit noted that it might need biopsy, but first he placed me on steroids to see if they would help reduce the size of the polyp.

They did not.

But still, truly, there seemed no imminent danger. I'd been living with this for ten years now. It was a constant nuisance, yes, but not a danger. It always came back benign, you see. Always.

On 26 June, in response to an invitation from Renaud Bombard, my publisher at Presses de la Cité in Paris, I sent this e-mail to him:

Dear Renaud:

First and foremost, yes! Dragica and I will be delighted to join you in Paris in January! I'll await further word from Sophie. Meanwhile, please tell her I know how we can save a lot of money on air fare.

Next, please tell Jacques Martinache I'm delighted that he'll be translating FAT OLLIE'S BOOK. He's a wonderful translator! I've already corrected the page proofs here, so I feel positive he'll have what he needs long before the summer is over. I will keep after S&S.

Meanwhile, I'll expect to hear from Sophie, and I look forward to seeing you both next January – which, after all, is not too very far away, is it?

All best, Evan

By 9 July, my voice had worsened considerably and the suspicious polyp had become an evil-looking white mass.

Two days later, Slavit did the biopsy.

'WELL, IT CAME BACK CANCER.'

16 July 2002, and Slavit uttering the words I shall never forget.

I swear to you, we were not negligent, we were watching it, we were minding the store, we were on the case, but the damn thing came back cancer, anyway.

On 23 July, in the year 2002, fully intending to remove the malignant growth and fold healthy skin from my neck onto my severely tested vocal cords, Blaugrund and Slavit aborted the operation when they realized the cancer had spread.

So the very next week, I was once again wheeled into the OR on a gurney, this time to have my entire larynx removed, and once again I heard my own voice intoning, backwards, 'Ten, nine, eight, seven . . .' until I got to six and couldn't remember anything anymore.

4

***

'NURSE, THERE'S A NOSTRIL IN MY THROAT!'

IN A MYSTERY NOVEL OF the sort I do not write, after the hero's been hit on the head from behind, he will later 'swim up through a sea of blackness' and blink his way toward consciousness. He will hear voices. The bad guys discussing their future plans. Whispers. Laughter. He is usually bound, sometimes gagged. He tries to figure out what happened to him, what is happening to him *now*, where he is, and to whom these strange voices might belong. Within minutes, it all comes clear to him.

I was in the Recovery Room at Lenox Hill Hospital. The voices belonged to Recovery Room nurses. One of the nurses laughed about something. Another nurse was complaining about her break time. Wasn't she supposed to have had a half-hour break sometime earlier? Yet another nurse clucked sympathetically. A telephone rang. A nurse told the caller that the patient wasn't ready to be moved yet. Was she talking about me? Had something gone wrong with the operation? What time was it? Where was Dina?

Something thick was stuck in my throat, a tube of some sort. I tried to cough it out. There was a smaller tube in my nose. The one in my nose hurt. There was yet another tube going into my right arm. There were fluids dripping into me from everywhere around the bed. There were machines beeping and little lights blinking. I tried to raise my head to get a better view of the room. I could not lift my head. I tried to call to one of the nurses. No voice came from my mouth.

The nurses kept scurrying about, babbling about everything but medical matters, everything but me.

It occurred to me that I'd had my larynx removed.

It occurred to me that I could not speak.

I almost began weeping.

Dina, I thought again. Where's Dina?

WHEN DR. BLAUGRUND FOUND ME, he was still in his operating gown. He wanted me to know that everything was fine, they had removed the cancer and Evan was doing well.

'Did you get it all?' I asked.

'Yes,' he said. 'All of it.'

I wanted to hug him, but instead I hugged myself.

'Thank you,' I said. 'Thank you, Dr. Blaugrund.'

The moment he left, I felt a current run through my body. I felt as if a giant frozen hand took possession of me and began to shake me violently. I hugged myself tight to stop the shaking but my knees gave way and I leaned on the wall so as not to fall. I felt myself sliding down, and some people came to help me. I remember holding on to a single thought, the urgency to call Amanda, and I asked if someone could please help me, could someone please find my address book? There was a dark cloud then, and a buzzing, and then the sound of distant voices, and the quiet of the room where they'd taken me to lie down. I don't know how long I was in that room, whimpering like a small injured animal.

I HAD FINALLY CAUGHT A nurse's eye.

She put her face close to mine and yelled, 'Yes, can I help you?'

I have since learned that when you cannot speak, people yell at you. They think you are deaf, not merely mute.

I signaled for a writing instrument. Held up my right hand like a pad, palm flat, mimed writing on it with my left hand.

'You want a pen?' the nurse yelled.

I nodded. It hurt when I nodded.

She came back with a pen, but no paper to write on.

On the palm of my hand I wrote:

Wife?

'You want your wife?' the nurse shouted.

I nodded again.

'He wants his wife!' she shouted to another nurse.

'Tell him she's outside,' the second nurse said.

'She's outside!' the first nurse shouted.

The second nurse leaned in over the bed. She hadn't been shouting until now, but now she yelled, 'How do you feel?'

I nodded that I was okay. I held up my right hand, showed her what I'd written there:

Wife?

'Your wife's okay!' she yelled. 'Don't worry about her!'

If I had a voice, I'd have yelled right back, 'But I *do* worry about her. I *am* worried about her. Where the fuck *is* she?'

Instead, I shook my head and pointed to my right hand again.

'We'll tell her you're okay!' she shouted. 'Are you in any pain?'

I shook my head.

Impatiently now, I kept stabbing at the palm of my right hand.

Wife?
Wife?
Wife?

The nurse walked off, shaking her head.

'Difficult patient,' I heard her telling someone.

DR. SLAVIT HAD COME LOOKING for me after I'd fainted, but he was now gone. I found Dr. Blaugrund in the corridor, and he invited me into his office. He made a drawing for me of exactly where on the vocal cords the cancer had been, and explained why they'd been unable to perform the other operation: the cancer had been growing underneath one of the cords and had partially invaded the other, healthy cord. It had also affected the cartilage, but had not gone through it.

'It's a very good thing that the larynx is out,' he told me.

'But are you sure all the *cancer* is out?'

'It is out, yes,' Dr. Blaugrund said.

They had removed it all, he told me, they had cut it all out – but of course, they would now have to wait for the pathology results.

I looked across the desk at him.

'You don't believe a word I'm saying, do you?' he asked.

I believed him, of course, but this was not what I wanted to hear. I did not want to live in fear that the cancer might still be there in some small dispersed cell, waiting for an opportune moment to attack again, to invade healthy tissue. I needed total assurance that with the removal of my husband's larynx, the cancer was gone, too. I needed a solid promise from Dr. Blaugrund – who had first looked at my husband's throat some ten years ago – that *this* time there was nothing to worry about, there'd be no more living in fear.

But this was exactly what this good doctor could not give me.

Seated at his desk, he explained gently that one could never turn his back on cancer, that Evan would have to be checked every month for the first year, then every three months in the second, every six in the third, and once a year after that. Only after five years had passed could he be considered cancer-free. I continued to look at him. I wanted to say, 'This isn't fair, my husband has lost his larynx, why can't we be free now?'

Dr. Blaugrund knew my thoughts.

'This is a tremendous loss for Evan,' he said. 'You'll have to be strong now, he'll need you. You must be positive now, your attitude will be very important to his recovery.'

For the second time that day, I thanked Dr. Blaugrund, and was on my way to the Recovery Room when I saw Amanda. She, too, had been trying to find out what was happening. No one had told her I'd been sent to another floor to wait for her father. No one at Reception was now able to tell us anything further, so Amanda and I decided to march into the Recovery Room on our own.

Almost all the patients from that room were gone now. Evan's bed was in the corner. At first, I was surprised at how good he looked. The color of his skin was a natural pink, and his breathing was calm, his chest moving in a regular rhythm. I had seen Evan after his heart attacks and after the triple-A operation, and I expected he'd look that way now, gray and in pain, or at least in discomfort. But not this time. No. He looked fine!

I took his hand.

'You're all right, darling,' I said. 'They got the cancer. Dr. Blaugrund told me they took it all out.'

Evan closed his eyes and nodded. His lips moved. They formed a perfect 'I know', but there was no sound. I could clearly see the hole in his neck and the plastic tube they'd placed in it, fastened with a white cotton string that went around his neck. There was no blood. Everything looked clean, pristine, almost festive, as if he'd put some kind of special tie on. I'd been afraid of this moment, of how I would react to the hole in my husband's throat, but I was now looking directly at it. Steam bubbled out of a blue tube in a tray that was hanging loosely over the opening. The steam made the little tray dance. With each breath that Evan took, the steam was drawn into the hole in his neck.

I felt sudden tenderness for this dark opening, perfectly

circled with a plastic ring. It seemed as if nothing had changed, none of this had actually happened. There was merely this new novelty of Evan breathing through a hole in his neck. I smiled at Evan. He smiled back. Amanda left the bedside to try to find someone who knew when he'd be moved to his private room. A nurse went by. I caught her eye.

'When is my husband going to be transferred to his room?' I asked.

'He isn't,' the nurse said. 'He's staying here for the night.'

'But I was told he'd leave the Recovery Room . . . we already have a private room . . .'

'No, he's not being moved yet.'

'Why not?'

'Because that's what the doctor ordered.'

'There must be some mistake,' I said. 'I've already spoken to the doctor, I was promised . . . they gave us a room . . . we booked a private nurse . . .'

'We can take better care of him on this floor,' the nurse said.

'Why? Is something wrong?'

'Nothing's wrong. He's staying here because that's what the doctor ordered.'

'Which doctor? His doctors are Slavit and Blaugrund, I feel sure they . . .'

'They're not here. And you'll have to leave now.'

'I'm not going to leave until I hear from his doctors that they want him to stay here overnight.'

Amanda had now joined me again. She'd found one of the young doctors who'd assisted Slavit and Blaugrund during the surgery. At first I thought he was the one who ordered that Evan remain here for the night. Not so. He began telling us how well the operation had gone. He praised the performance of the two surgeons, these two maestros joined in a perfect operatic act, he explained how smooth and clean

... 'There was no blood, hardly any...' He mentioned the precision of the cuts the two veteran surgeons had made ... 'Such a performance! Such perfection!' All the doctors observing and assisting the two surgeons, including himself, had a hard time concentrating on their own tasks, they were drawn to watch...

His conversation became more and more directed to Amanda, maybe because I was too distressed, maybe because her knowledge of medications and anesthesiology was greater than mine, or maybe simply because she was so very beautiful. The doctor was tall and redheaded. Standing beside Amanda, tall herself, dark-haired and slender, it occurred to me that they would make a nice couple.

They continued to chat. I stood apart like a bystander, still not hearing why Evan was being kept here. I interrupted to ask if he knew why. His answer was the same one the nurse had given us.

'It's better for him to remain here. It'll be safer if there's any problem.'

'*Is* there a problem?'

'No, everything's all right.'

'Then why can't he be released?'

He really did not have any answer to that. I asked to talk to either Dr. Blaugrund or Dr. Slavit, and when they all realized that I wasn't going to leave until I talked to one or the other of the surgeons, they finally connected me to Dr. Slavit. He seemed surprised that Evan was still in the Recovery Room, but assured me that it would be all right if he remained there for the night. He didn't give me any specific reason for this, but I got the feeling he didn't want to interfere with the resident doctor or whoever else was here on the floor. He tried to calm me by saying that the Recovery Room would be a doctor's preference after surgery, anyway, but that not all patients could afford this.

'It's a much better environment,' he said. 'Cleaner, bacteria free.'

But I still was not given a clear reason why almost everyone else operated on at the same time as my husband had left the Recovery Room long ago. I probably would have persisted if I'd been alone, but being there with Amanda, I let her make the decision, and she and the redheaded doctor agreed to leave Evan there for the night. The doctor promised us that he'd be moved to a more comfortable bed than the one he'd been wheeled in on from the operating room. He further promised that a quieter area would be created for him so that he could rest comfortably during the night.

'I think he'll be all right,' Amanda said gently, and reluctantly I agreed to leave.

We would later learn why Evan had been detained in the Recovery Room. The decision was made by a young doctor monitoring Evan's heart, uncertain what effect the anesthesia might have had on what he perceived as an 'abnormal' reading. I still don't know who this doctor was, but if he had contacted Evan's cardiologist, or had taken the time to look at Evan's chart, he would have realized that a so-called lower-left bundle branch block was a quite normal condition of my husband's heart. It had always been that way, and it had never caused any trouble. If he had talked to me, I would have told him that. He had not spoken to me or to Evan's cardiologist. And all that night, he remained invisible.

In the corridor outside the Recovery Room, I was stopped by a nurse I'd never seen before.

'I saw you when they brought you into that room to collect yourself,' she said. 'I see you're still here! Your husband's not the only one who ever lost his larynx, you know. My brother's just been diagnosed with cancer, but I'm here, I'm working, life goes on. Go eat something!'

I could not tell if she was a friend or an enemy.

A NURSE LEANED IN OVER my bed.

'Your room is ready now,' she shouted.

I lowered my eyes in a silent sarcastic *Thank you*.

As she walked away from the bed, I heard her whisper to another nurse, 'Go tell The Immigrant.'

I KNOW THAT DINA'S ACCOUNT of what happened that night is a true and accurate one, but I sometimes wonder if my own nightmare experience in the Recovery Room might have been drug-inspired. I was, after all, coming up out of anesthesia. I had, after all, been unconscious on an operating table for six hours. So perhaps the nurses were discussing a severely broken leg rather than a coffee break. Perhaps I only imagined them labeling my wife 'The Immigrant'. Considering the Babel of foreign accents in that room, this particular epithet would have been unseemly, anyway. But I know for certain that I heard a doctor ask, in plain English, 'Is it always so noisy in here?' and I know I heard in response the delighted giggles of clueless nurses.

Then again . . .

I remember being moved to a basement room without windows . . .

'No such room exists,' Dina told me later.

. . . a cheerless room with a pair of twin beds . . .

'No, darling, there was no such room.'

. . . covered with maroon chenille bedspreads.

'You were dreaming.'

In which case, did I dream Dina making repeated calls – from an old-fashioned black telephone on an ornate night table between the beds – to the private nurse who was supposed to be waiting for me immediately after the operation? And didn't I fall asleep again on one of those twin beds while Dina slept on the other, reaching across the abyss to hold my hand? And didn't a nurse come in to wake me up and take my temperature or my blood? And didn't a strange doctor in a white tunic with a stethoscope in his pocket lean over the bed and ask how I was doing?

'No, darling,' Dina told me later. 'They moved you directly to the room Pavarotti had when he stayed here.'

Did I ask at the time, 'But why? I'll never sing again, you know.'

I TOLD HIM, 'YOU'RE CANCER free, my honey.'

He was still heavily sedated.

He looked into my face. He nodded. His lips formed the silent word *Good*.

I began to reassure him further, telling him that Dr. Blaugrund had told me they were able to take out all the cancer, and were very happy with the results.

I told him he was going to be okay, we were going to be okay.

He nodded again.

I AM SUDDENLY A BIGGER star than Pavarotti.

This was still – and always would be – Pavarotti's Room, but there was no question about who now commanded all the attention here. Evan Hunter had entered the scene, center stage, and the spotlight was on me – or, more accurately, my throat.

First thing in the morning, after the obligatory temperature and blood-pressure readings were taken, a nurse administered the 'Mucomyst Treatment'. Since I could no longer breathe through my nose or my mouth, a mask was placed over the hole in my throat, which I still had not grown accustomed to calling a stoma. This mask was attached to a tube, which in turn ran into a 'nebulizer' machine alongside the bed. (It sounds like science fiction, I know.) A fine mist

114

traveled into my throat and induced coughing, attributable this time to the medication and not any reflex mechanism. Or so I understood. Actually, I was pushing the morphine-release button whenever I was in pain, and could barely focus on what they were doing to me. But Dina was paying close attention. And this is how she saw it:

'I noticed that a small tube was attached to a pressure bottle on the wall. The nurse injected medication mixed with saline into a tray that was attached to this tube. She fastened this tray over the stoma, and adjusted the pressure valve until bubbles started to form and a steamy mixture entered Evan's lungs, causing him to begin coughing. Over a period of about ten minutes, the steam mixture would evaporate while Evan kept coughing up as much mucus as he possibly could. I was told that this was very important for the health of the lungs. Everyone was concerned that there be no danger of pneumonia.'

After my Mucomyst Treatment, a nurse went into my throat with a plastic tube attached to a suction machine. She twirled this tube around inside as if she were beating eggs, sucking up unwanted mucus and drying blood and necrotic debris and what-not, seemingly oblivious to the fact that her violent stirrings triggered a cough reflex that caused hacking paroxysms.

Dina remembers it this way:

'From the first time I witnessed the suctioning, I was terrified of it. Sometimes, Evan would have a brief respite between the Mucomyst routine and the suctioning; the nurses all seemed overworked, no matter what time of day or night it was, and they were always running off to look after another patient. Either that or the Mucomyst had irritated my husband's lungs so drastically and caused such extensive coughing that the nurses would have to give him a few moments' rest before the next ordeal.

'Usually, and depending on the nurse who was on duty, I

would exchange a few diplomatic words with her, trying to present Evan's case to her without offending her capabilities, asking her to please be careful and gentle with him. But in the end, whoever the nurse was, I simply got out of her way, tense and frightened of what was lying just ahead. Tension, I later realized, was the way I dealt with much of the fear and pain my husband's sickness brought.'

ALL OF THIS SUCTIONING AND Mucomysting also succeeds in getting me wet more often than not. Wet. Yes. It is not supposed to do this, I suppose, but the tubes always seem to be popping out of their connections, unexpectedly spraying my neck or my face or both with cold water. This causes me to jerk away from each new sudden shower. This causes my throat and my nose to hurt all over again.

I do not wish to be wet. But everything in Medland seems either vaguely damp or frankly wet. There appears to be a persistent drip somewhere, and I can't locate the source of it because I can't turn my head. Am I bleeding? Did I wet the bed? Is there a leak in the ceiling? The air conditioner? The suction machine? The toilet? Where? Everything is just out of reach, either beyond my line of vision, or below it, or above it, or behind it. Or somewhere. But where? The nebulizer? Wherever or whatever it is, you can bet that by the time the nurse finishes the Mucomysting, I will not only be wet, but I will also have coughed myself into exhaustion.

It is all part of the healing process.

I guess.

THE DOCTORS THREE ARRIVE *EN MASSE* sometime later in the morning. There is a palpable air of expectation and excitement on the floor just prior to their arrival. It reminds me somehow – I can't imagine why – of the fear and anticipation attendant on the Commodore's weekly inspection when I was in boot camp fifty-eight years ago. There are no white gloves here to check for dust on your polished black shoes. Instead, there are white tunics. And stethoscopes, of course. But the nurses and the nurses' aides and even the guy mopping the floor in the toilet all stand at attention when the Doctors Three enter the room and genially ask how I'm feeling this morning.

I nod and smile.

How am I feeling? I am feeling as if my throat is swollen and painful, and for some strange reason my nose hurts, too, (yes, my *nose*) and I am coughing as if I have tuberculosis. That is how I am feeling.

The doctors look into my throat.

My throat is the star here. The rest of my body is merely attached to it. If my throat survives this ordeal, I too will survive. It is as simple as that. I am made to understand (though not *why*) that pneumonia is – if not exactly an imminent danger – at least a definite possibility. You do not want to get pneumonia, they tell me. Pneumonia will not be good for you. Which is why they now pay such close attention to my lungs, listening with their stethoscopes and then nodding, and telling me that everything sounds fine so far. The words 'so far' sound ominous so far. I want everything to sound fine and look fine and *be* fine forever. I want to get out of here as soon as possible, and I never want to see another hospital as long as I live.

This is a prison movie.

I want to pass a note to Dina with the scribbled words *The break is set for tonight!*

THE NURSE FROM HELL RIDES her broomstick into Pavarotti's Room at a little after dusk, on the day after I lost my larynx, my voice and – it seemed to me then – my unique identity.

She is black and gaunt, this horror, and she is leading a coven of ten or twelve other witches who are there to change my bedsheets and my bedclothes before the changing of the guard. (Actually, there is only the Weird Sister herself, and one other nurse, this one white. But just now I am on a morphine drip, and to me they are a horde, and flames are roaring from their nostrils and mouths, and smoke is hissing from their ears.)

Dina is as alarmed as I am.

'May I help?' she asks.

'You go away,' the black nurse tells her. 'Can he stand? Get up!' she tells me. 'We have to change the bed. What's wrong with him?' she shouts. She leans over the bed. 'What's wrong with you?' she shouts into my face. 'Stand up! We have to change the bed!'

Both nurses grab for the sheets under me as if getting ready to toss me into the air. Defensively, I reach for the tube stitched into my nose. My other hand is flapping on the covers, searching for C.C. Wong's blackboard.

'Lift your head!' the black nurse commands.

It is difficult for me to move into a sitting position without help. My larynx is gone, and with it much of my lifting power. I cannot move my neck without experiencing pain. I cannot lift my head. I cannot sit up. I grab for my own hair, clutch a handful of it in my fist, pull on it, trying to demonstrate that my head must be lifted for me, I cannot do it by myself.

The black nurse is about to yank the pillow from under my head.

Dina steps between her and the bed.

'He can't lift his head!' she shouts. 'He had a laryngectomy!'

'He can lift his *legs*, can't he?' the white nurse asks, and yanks back the sheet. Together, they discover that both my legs are fastened to the bed, enclosed in inflatable leggings to prevent blood clotting. Pondering this, they loosen the bindings, and lift my legs, exposing my ass for all the world to see. Standing stiff and straight in their starched white uniforms, each wearing a crucifix around her neck, heads together, they debate for a moment how best they can accomplish their mission of mercy. And then they become a silently efficient bed-changing machine, black hands and white hands moving swiftly and effectively, stripping the bed and smoothing the wrinkles out of the clean sheets. The black nurse comes to the head of the bed again. Ignoring me, she reaches for the pillow.

I point my finger at her.

I point it like a revolver.

'What is he trying to say?' she asks Dina.

I mouth the word *You!*

She blinks at me.

I mouth the word *Out!*

She blinks again.

I mouth both words together. *You! Out!*

My eyes are a yellow laserbeam.

I sweep my hand toward the door, banishing her.

She stares at me wordlessly.

Then she says, 'God bless you.'

It is a curse.

On my little blackboard, I write: **WILL THEY BE BACK?**

'Over my dead body,' Dina says.

THE LITTLE BLACKBOARD C.C. WONG was reluctant to give me on the night of our so-called farewell party is one of these children's learning tools. It is called Magna-Doodle, and it is manufactured by Fisher-Price, and it is a cutely designed little thing, all purply and white, with a little yellow plastic knob set into a track that runs along the bottom of its frame. The frame itself encloses a white plastic screen with what I guess is some sort of graphite solution under it. (Science has never been my strong suit. In college, I filled the science requirement by taking a course in Geology. Does that tell you anything?) There is a little depression on the right-hand side of the purple frame, and a yellow plastic tool that looks like a crayon fits into this cavity.

There is no slate here as such.

There is no chalk, either.

There is only the white plastic screen and the yellow plastic crayon.

But when I write on that screen with that crayon, whatever I write appears on the screen in black.

Magic!

And when I pull that little plastic knob across the track on the bottom, the writing disappears, clearing the screen for subsequent writing.

More magic!

Magic and more magic are sure as hell what I need in this hospital room.

DINA IS PART OF THE MAGIC.

When I write *I LOVE YOU* on the blackboard, it is as if I dropped rubies and pearls at her feet. She smiles radiantly, and hugs me close, and in her broken tongue . . .

'Come, your answer in broken music! For thy voice is music and thy English broken . . .'

. . . she marvels extravagantly about the wonders of C.C.'s gift, and urges me to write something else for her.

EVAN AND I BEGAN TO chat, sharing the board at first. Then we both realized that I could talk, and our conversation continued, catching each other's thoughts, giving answers to unfinished sentences, familiar with each other's feelings, I speaking, Evan writing, intimate in our pain, happy to be able to share it with each other.

I told Evan of the fear I'd gone through during these last two days, of my ordeal at the door of the recovery room. He told me of the treatment he'd received there, and the opinion the nurses had held of me.

We talked about this beautiful room, once Pavarotti's, now ours, and the time we would have to spend here. We talked . . . and talked . . . and talked . . . until my husband began to get drowsy again and drifted off. I wrote the words *CANCER FREE* on the board, and propped it on the table so that it would be visible when he opened his eyes again. Then I left him to sleep behind the curtains.

Not once had he mentioned the loss of his larynx.

We *will* be okay, I thought.

THE THROAT INSIDE MY NECK is presently a mass of raw and healing tissue, which is why it hurts so much, and causes me to hit the morphine-release button as often as I do. I have been assured that I won't become the Barney Ross of the literary world; the machine won't allow me to order morphine in sufficient amounts to make me an addict. But it is neither my throat nor the hole in my neck that is causing the most pain. It is the now-useless appendage . . .

You see, the larynx serves as a sort of railroad switch. When you swallow food, the larynx allows it to pass through the esophagus into the stomach. When you breathe, the larynx closes the switch on the esophagus track, opens the switch on the windpipe track, and expresses air into your lungs.

However—

You no longer have a larynx.

There is no longer a friendly switchman standing at the food–air switch to speed trains onto their proper tracks.

When they remove your larynx, the surgeons create two separate sets of tracks, in effect, one for food, the other for air. You no longer breathe through your nose or your mouth. In fact, once your throat heals, the primary purpose of your mouth will be to accept food, chew it, and swallow it. Right now, you are breathing through the healing wound in your throat, which is held open by a metal, elbow-shaped tube an inch or so in diameter.

The body seeks to heal wounds, to close them up. The trach tube is there to make sure this doesn't happen, to keep the hole open while permanent scar tissue forms around it. The tube is only temporary. The way you breathe from now on is not. You are now, and will forever be, a so-called neck breather. Understand that. You will never again breathe through your mouth or your nose. Your mouth is there to process food. Your nose no longer filters or moistens air. It is at best an ornament, a useless meaty *appurtenance* on your face.

But it is this worthless accessory, this beak, this proboscis, this schnoz, this goddamn *nose* that is now causing me excruciating pain.

This *what*?

Well, figure it out.

If my throat is healing, how can I swallow food?

I can't. Forget it. I will rip out all the stitches, I will cause hemorrhaging, alarms will sound and nurses will come running from all over Medland.

But if I expect to heal, I need nourishment, don't I? I have to eat, don't I? I mean ... isn't that so?

Well ... sure.

I guess.

But how can I eat if I can't swallow?

Easy.

I can eat through my nose.

(Well, gee, doesn't everyone?)

122

There is a tube in my nose, you see. And I am being fed liquid nourishment through this tube. There is a plastic bag hanging from a stainless steel pole beside the bed, and the nurses put up a new bag three times a day, at feeding time, and the bag empties into the tube in my nose, which bypasses my raw and healing throat, and goes directly through my esophagus and into my stomach.

So why does eating through my nose hurt so goddamn much?

Because the tube is *stitched* into my nostril.

Why is the tube *stitched* into my nostril?

Because everyone was fearful that the tube might accidentally pull free, ripping the stitches, and forcing them to open my throat all over again.

Which can mean serious trouble.

'You don't want that to happen,' I've been warned.

Meanwhile, I am the one with the feeding tube stitched into my right nostril.

Whenever this tube moves even the slightest fraction of an inch, whenever it is accidentally touched, or even gingerly moved aside by a nurse administering to whatever my current need may be, pain rockets from my nostril into my head and I want to scream aloud if only I had a voice. Barney Ross would have known just how much getting punched in the nose hurts. Every prize fighter knows that you 'go for the nose' not only because it bleeds so easily but because it hurts so much to get *punched* there.

Well, I am getting punched in the nose a dozen times a day, and nobody in the ring with me seems even remotely aware of the unintentional abuse. Each time I leap for the ceiling, a surprised nurse spreads her hands in shocked innocence. So I figure I'd better keep an eye on the referee, because I'm sure as hell losing this fight.

In self defense, I hand-letter a sign and ask Dina to tack it to the cork bulletin board hanging on the wall to the left of the bed. The sign reads:

DO NOT TOUCH THIS PATIENT'S NOSE!!!!!

So now, whenever a nurse approaches the bed, I give her my evil, yellow, laserbeam stare, and Dina politely asks her to read the sign. The nurse returns a bemused look, but she doesn't touch me anywhere on the face because she realizes I will sever her hand from the wrist if she makes the slightest move toward my precious goddamn nose.

IT IS IRONIC THAT MY 'overnight fame' came with *The Blackboard Jungle* when I was twenty-eight years old, and I am now almost seventy-six and scribbling on a blackboard in Pavarotti's Room. I become adept – too adept, one might say – very quickly. My dexterity dates back to when I was on a Navy destroyer in the middle of the Pacific during World War II. I did not win the war single-handedly. In fact, the war was over when we sailed for Japan. But as part of my radarman duties, I was required to stand behind a big clear Plexiglas sheet, writing on it backwards. Yes, backwards. So that it could be read from the other side. Wearing earphones, I would take ranges and bearings from whoever in the radar gang was manning the Sugar George or Sugar Roger gear, mark the position with a big X on the Plexiglas, and then letter the time alongside it backwards, so that it could be read by the CIC officer who would then translate the jottings into a course and speed, thereby avoiding accidental collisions and such. CIC stood for Combat Information Center. But the war was over, and we had nothing else to do with our time.

'What goes around comes around.'

This was a favorite expression of my movie agent, Gary

Salt – who only three years earlier had died when his colon cancer metastasized and spread into his bones. Now I am in a hospital room, having had my larynx removed so that *I* won't die of cancer, and I am writing backwards the way I'd been trained to do in the Navy more than half a century ago.

I hold the blackboard facing my no doubt breathlessly expectant audience.

I letter the words backwards, so that (to me at least) the message seems to unfold naturally from left to right, where it can be read plainly and with ease by whoever is on the other side of the board.

Just like old times.

The Doctors Three are enormously impressed with my writing skill, which by the time of their next visit has progressed to writing not only backwards but upside down as well.

They are not as easily impressed with my lungs.

A NURSE'S AIDE WHEELS THE chair into my room shortly after I've ingested through my nose the sixteen ounces of Ensure that is my daily breakfast. In Medland-shorthand she asks simply, 'X-ray?' and I nod, and she asks, 'Is it okay for you to get out of bed?' and I nod again, and she gives me a somewhat dubious look.

I am still attached to the morphine-dispensing apparatus, and I still have an IV in my arm, and the ever-present, ever-painful feeding tube still runs up into my nose and down into my stomach. So it takes a bit of maneuvering (and a lot of help from Dina and the day nurse) before I can clamber out of bed without tangling or disconnecting the IV, and without touching or twisting the pain-producing nose tube. When I am finally seated in the chair, Dina kisses me on the cheek, tells me she's going to run down for some breakfast, and promises to be waiting for me when I come back.

I've been in other wheelchairs before this morning, of course, being transported to or from one section of a hospital to another, after one procedure or another, even being wheeled down to my car after being signed out of this or that hospital in Norwalk or Bridgeport or Cleveland or Baltimore, or New York, or wherever – so yes, I've been in other wheelchairs before.

This morning is different.

Understand please, I have no real desire to make small talk with the aide pushing the wheelchair, no dire need to exchange pleasantries with any of the doctors, nurses or other patients who enter and then quit the elevator. Trains that pass in the night, right? Strangers when we meet.

But during all those other procedures, nothing was taken from my body. My body remained intact. This time – on 30 July, two days ago to be precise – something was indeed taken from me. My larynx was excised. And sitting in that wheelchair on the first day of August, listening to the babble of voices in the elevator, I suddenly miss with all my heart that two-inch segment of anatomy, and the singular voice it once generated.

I am silent all the way down to the basement.

The X-ray departments of hospitals are always in the basement. Or maybe not. Maybe it just *seems* that in a hospital only the patients' rooms are above ground, whereas everything else to do with the black art of medicine is hidden in subterranean chambers, secret and apart. Hospitals are frightening places. In hospitals, they cut you open. They take off your arms and legs. They remove your larynx. They make it impossible for you to bid 'Good morning' to strangers in an elevator.

I've since been told that the Radiology Department at Lenox Hill Hospital is on the third floor. I did not know where it was on that day I went down for my chest X-ray. I remember the nurse's aide wheeling me out of the elevator into yet another corridor that felt very much like a basement corridor – well, it *had* to be in the basement, don't you think? I mean, I couldn't be hallucinating yet another windowless basement room, could I? This was now Post-Three, I'd had my surgery two full days ago. So, *yes* then, the aide wheeled me into a basement corridor teeming with hospital personnel and patients, where she left me facing a blank wall while she went off to inform someone or other that the patient from Pavarotti's Room was here for his chest X-ray.

Facing a blank wall.

A patient from *Pavarotti's* Room!

I still could not turn my head without enormous difficulty.

I sat in that wheelchair, staring at the wall in that basement corridor and wondered why the aide might have thought I'd actually prefer facing a wall instead of watching the passing scene.

Sitting there in an invalid's wheelchair, wearing an invalid's short striped hospital gown, looking at the wall and hearing behind me people using their voices the way I would never again be able to use mine. I suddenly felt trapped in a nightmare world I had no desire to inhabit. I knew it would not take a rocket scientist to figure out how to turn that wheelchair, knew that with a few tries I could probably maneuver the chair so that I was no longer facing the wall, but for a moment . . .

Two moments.

Three.

A frozen eternity.

I sat there helplessly facing the wall, unable to cry out for assistance, unable to explain that perhaps I could not speak but that didn't mean a person had to leave me facing the fucking *wall*, did it?

It *did* take a rocket scientist.

I turned first this wheel and then the other one. I kept banging my toes into the wall. I was not wearing shoes. In

Medland, they take away your shoes, and give you paper slippers for your feet. Everything else is either hard and immovable or else on wheels so that with relative ease you can repeatedly bang your toes into things or have them run over. I kept turning the wheels. Finally, I managed to rotate the chair a full 180 degrees.

There was a busy hum of conversation not mine.

There were other people waiting in wheelchairs, talking.

There were other people sitting on benches, talking.

There were doctors or nurses or technicians or whatever the hell they were, talking, moving in and out of rooms, talking, walking up and down the corridor, talking, carrying clipboards or folders, talking, all of them talking.

I recognized the nurse's aide who'd wheeled me down here. She came striding up the corridor, talking to someone, looking around as if she'd lost me. When finally she spotted me, she came over with a cheerful smile, dropped a folder into my lap, and said, 'Someone'll be with you shortly. They'll call when you need to be taken up again.' And she walked off.

I waited for an hour or more in that corridor.

I kept signaling to anyone I thought might be able to tell me how long it would be before I could have my chest X-rayed because I might have pneumonia here, you know, and that would not be good for me, you know.

Everyone seemed so very busy.

The hospital corridor had suddenly turned into a French restaurant. No one saw me gesturing. Or if they did, they ignored me. Besides, if I had something to say, why didn't I simply say it instead of sitting there waving my hands around like a dummy?

I began realizing that I could sit in that basement corridor forever . . .

Yes, damn it, it *was* a basement!

And yes, damn it, it *had* been forever!

... sit there through all eternity in my short, bare-legged nightgown with my ass and my paper-slippered feet hanging out, sit in that damn invalid's wheelchair till doomsday, and no one would come to ask what I was doing here until and unless I could make my impatience and my displeasure known, until I could vent what I now realized was a monumental anger that had been building for the past three days now.

I could not yell, I could not scream, I could only make an angry face and wave frantically to a young man rushing past in blue scrubs. To my great surprise, he stopped. I gestured to my throat, mouthed silent words, shook my head so he'd know I couldn't speak. I gestured to my chest, then crossed my forefingers, forming an X, letting him know I was there for an X-ray, and not merely waiting for my baggage to be unloaded from a plane at Kennedy Airport.

He said, 'How long have you been waiting here?'

I rolled my eyes.

'What's your name?' he asked, and picked up the folder in my lap. He studied it, nodded, and said, 'Let me see what's happening, okay?'

Ten minutes later, somebody wheeled me into a room with an X-ray machine, and a technician apologized to me for the long wait, and at last they took the X-rays.

That morning, I learned that unless I was very, very careful, I would be forever dependent upon the kindness of strangers.

I AM BEING TUBE-FED six cans of Ensure every day.

Each can is an eight-ounce serving similar to the one you can buy in your local health food store, except that this one is prepared especially for hospitals, and it doesn't come in different flavors because you can't taste it, anyway. Each can contains 300 calories of a thick tasteless nutrition-rich fluid.

The nurse pops the can, pours the liquid into the bedside bag, and then thins it with water so that it will flow slowly but easily down to the stomach through the tube in the nose.

I support the tube carefully as the liquid moves through it because if it is jostled or jarred, I will shriek in silent pain.

I do not enjoy this feeding process.

You have to understand that being fed through the nose is not the same thing as enjoying a steak in a fancy restaurant. There is no pleasure at all attached to the experience. After you've been fed both cans of Ensure, you do not feel as if you've just had a pleasant dining experience. You don't even feel 'full' as in 'satisfied'. Your *stomach* feels full, yes, you can actually feel the liquid moving through the tube into your stomach, you can feel your stomach taking in this thick liquid, but when it's all over and done with, you don't feel 'full', you don't feel as if you've just eaten, you don't feel as if you've just had a meal. You feel as if something has been poured down your nose into your stomach, that is how you feel.

On her shift last night, the nurse had trouble getting the first can of Ensure to go down. But she'd been here before, believe me, there is not much the experienced nurses on this floor haven't seen or heard before. Whenever the Ensure doesn't want to go down the tube, it means it's too thick and what you do is thin it down. That is what you do. You open a bottle of sterile water, and you pour it slowly into the bag of Ensure hanging there uncooperatively beside the bed. But this time, it *still* took a very long while for the fluid to drip into the tube, so the night nurse decided to postpone feeding me the *second* can of Ensure until much later in her shift. She diluted this one with water, too. It, too, took a very long time to drip down into my belly. But at last, I'd been fed the equivalent of *four* cans of liquid – the Ensure plus the water – rather than two.

Fade out.

The morning nurse comes on.

Once again, the Ensure seems to be taking an inordinately long time to make the journey from my nose to my stomach. The nurse is concerned. Is something blocking the tube? She starts to fiddle with the tube, and I wave my hands *No!*, and point to the sign on the bulletin board, and she nods acknowledgement, she has been here before, she knows all about my goddamn nose. But the fluid isn't flowing the way it should, it is not pouring down my nose. This morning, it is just sitting there, obstinately refusing to move as freely as it normally does.

Well, she's been *here* before, too.

She checks my stomach with a stethoscope.

'I can hear it moving in there,' she says. 'It's beginning to come down.'

Convinced that everything is now as it should be, she leaves the room to tend to other patients.

Dina is sitting on the couch across from the bed, thumbing through a magazine, when all at once I start coughing. She looks up. She is not alarmed. I cough all the time.

But suddenly I am throwing up.

Nothing is supposed to be passing through my throat.

Nothing.

Not in either direction.

Neither down *nor* up.

Certainly, nothing is supposed to be heaving convulsively past stitches and healing tissue, nothing is supposed to be violently jetting from my mouth onto my chin and my hands and my gown and all over the pillows and the sheets.

Dina is on her feet and yelling down the hall. 'Help! My husband is throwing up! Come help him! Please!'

A nurse is there in an instant.

An instant later, the resident is there.

And an instant after that, Blaugrund is in my room.

'How much did he throw up?' he asks Dina.

'Everything they fed him.'

'I don't like this,' he says. 'If he tore his sutures . . .'

He lets the sentence dangle. He leans over the bed. He puts a light in my throat. He is silent for a long while, looking.

'It's all right,' he says at last. 'They overfed you, the food overflowed. But the sutures are all right, everything's all right.' He snaps off the light. 'You were very lucky,' he tells me.

I do not feel very lucky.

IT IS NOW MONDAY, THE fifth day of August, six days after surgery was performed to remove my larynx – 'Post-Six', as the day is commemorated in Medland.

The feeding tube is still stitched into my nostril.

There is no longer any pain in my throat. The only pain is in my fucking nose. Moreover, after throwing up yesterday, I now have the hiccups. I feel like the Pope, except that when he had the hiccups, he didn't also have a tube stitched into his nose. Every time I hiccup – which is once every minute or so – the tube moves ever so slightly. And each time I soundlessly shriek at the excruciating pain.

I am becoming obsessed with the tube.

Perhaps that is its purpose.

To cause me to forget that I no longer have a larynx.

I have begun putting the same question to every nurse who walks into the room:

'What are the chances that a feeding tube *not* stitched into the nostril will slip out of place and cause trouble? One in a hundred? 500? 5000? One in 10,000?'

At first, they all hem and haw.

Is this a trick question?

Finally, they come clean.

In all their years of experience . . .

Twenty years, ten years, five years, it varies . . .

... there were maybe one or two hallucinating or aggressive patients who ripped out their feeding tubes. Never have any of the nurses known a tube to slip out of place accidentally.

When the doctors come to make their daily rounds that morning, I tell them on my writing pad that I can no longer tolerate this stitching in my nose, which now seems to have been totally unnecessary in the first place.

I am told, 'Well, you wouldn't have wanted us to go in again, believe me.'

I write: *I FEEL LIKE A BULL WITH A RING IN HIS NOSE.*

They say, 'Well,' and nod sympathetically.

Referring to my vomiting the day before, Blaugrund tells me again how lucky I was, and says, 'We want to be cautious here.'

Slavit tells a story about a laryngectomee who got released from the hospital and went to eat a cheeseburger that very same day.

'He tore all the sutures in his throat,' he says, nodding. 'We had to do the operation all over again. It took him three weeks to recover this time.'

I write: *WHEN ARE THESE STITCHES IN MY NOSE COMING OUT?*

Blaugrund says, 'Maybe we can take our chances in a few days. Certainly no sooner than that.'

I write: *I'VE BEEN HERE BEFORE, YOU'VE SAID THAT BEFORE. WHEN IS SOON? WHEN ARE THEY COMING OUT?*

'We'll have to see,' he tells me. 'Meanwhile, we'll give you medication for those hiccups.'

The anesthesiologist who refused to let me out of the Recovery Room stands by nodding his head in silent sympathetic agreement.

I am beginning to hate them all.

They are my torturers.

They are the thieves who stole my larynx.

133

A WOMAN I'VE NEVER SEEN before comes grinning and jiggling and bouncing into Pavarotti's Room not twenty minutes later.

'Ed McBain?' she says.

She is perhaps twenty-five or -six years old, a shapely black woman wearing a short tight skirt and a clinging rust-colored blouse that swoops low over what can only be called exuberant breasts. She is not wearing a bra. Even Dina's eyes pop.

Without waiting for an answer, she takes my right hand between both hers, and says, 'I have read *each* and *every* one of your books, and I am *so* happy to meet you at last.'

I am not in the mood for visitors. I have just been told by the Doctors Three that the feeding tube will be staying in my nose for at least a few more days.

Still holding my hand, she sits on the edge of the bed, and – like a relative discussing our mutual family – asks if I think Steve Carella will ever cheat on his wife . . .

'He better not,' she warns, squeezing my hand and scowling.

. . . asks whether that poor boy Kling will ever find happiness with a good woman . . .

'Do you think Sharyn Cooke is right for him?' she asks solemnly. 'I know she's a sistuh, but I'm not too sure about her, uh-uh.'

. . . asks if I think Fat Ollie Weeks will ever stop being such a terrible bigot . . .

'I think there may be hope for him yet, don't you?' she asks, and squeezes my hand again. 'Though he *is* such a wretch, ain't he?'

She tells me she wishes the Deaf Man would come back in another book . . .

'Though I hope this time they catch him . . .'

. . . tells me that the time Carella got shot so long ago, she almost closed the book and stopped reading for fear he would die.

'I'm so glad he didn't,' she says, 'aren't you?'

She tells me she was on her way home this morning after having been on all night, when one of the other nurses on the floor told her I was here in Pavarotti's Room. She says she's been working the other end of the floor this past week, otherwise she'd have known earlier I was here and stopped by to say hello.

'Are you all right?' she asks me, leaning close and looking into my eyes. 'What'd they do to you, anyway?'

Dina explains that they discovered cancer in my throat and had to remove my larynx.

She nods knowingly, and then says, 'But they got it, right? They killed the cancer.'

On my blackboard, I write *YES, THEY KILLED THE CANCER.*

'So that's okay then, right?' she says. 'You'll be out of here in no time, writing your books again. You ought to have Hal Willis meet somebody nice, he's been mourning too long over that Marilyn girl, you know whut I'm saying? Maybe he could hook up with Eileen Burke, I *love* that woman's hair! I almost went to the beauty parlor one time t'have my own hair done like hers, how you think I'd look with fire-engine hair, oh *man!*' she says, and bursts out laughing.

Squeezing my hand again, she leans over the bed to hug me. 'So okay then, everything's fine here, right?' she says, and rises, and smoothes her skirt, and thrusts out her magnificent chest, and says, 'You take care now, Ed, you hear?' and goes jiggling and bouncing and grinning out of the room.

I look at C.C. Wong's blackboard.

I read the writing there.

YES, THEY KILLED THE CANCER.

Dina is staring at me.

I smile.

I nod.

She nods back.

So here we are.

KEVIN SMITH IS MY EDITOR at Pocket Books, Inc.

On that sixth day Post-Op, he comes to visit me. He is perhaps in his early forties, some five-feet-nine inches tall, with a good head of hair, and a moustache he's had since he was much younger. He goes to the gym on a regular basis, and he runs every day, and over the past several months, we have come to know each other quite well. I can't quite define the quality of the relationship. Kevin says I'm like an older brother to him. To me, he is like a caring son. But now that I can no longer speak, I wonder if our relationship will be as good as it was in the past.

These days I wonder about this a lot. I wonder if people will continue to see in me the Evan who used to be, or will they now see merely an old man fumbling with a blackboard and a plastic crayon?

I am determined not to make this sickness turn me into an old man.

But what sickness?

Hey, the cancer is gone, isn't it?

Well, yes. But . . .

I am here in a hospital full of sick people.

I am writing on a child's blackboard.

I am sick.

'You look terrific!' Kevin tells me at once. 'I didn't expect you to look this great.'

'His recuperative powers are amazing,' Dina says. 'Even the doctors are surprised.'

'I mean it, Evan,' Kevin says. 'You really look wonderful!'

On the blackboard, I letter the words *DO YOU THINK THERE'S A BOOK IN ALL THIS?*

This is the first time I've fielded the possibility.

Without hesitation, Kevin answers, 'Absolutely!' And then, again without hesitation, he adds, 'But don't write it upside down and backwards.'

We all burst out laughing.

JANE GELFMAN COMES TO VISIT at the end of the day.

On a lined pad, I outline a rectangle. Into the rectangle, I letter the words:

> *NURSE,*
> *THERE'S A NOSTRIL IN*
> *MY THROAT*
>
> *a memoir by*
>
> *EVAN HUNTER*

Dina begins smiling at once. Even though she recognizes that I'm seriously proposing a future book, she also realizes I've just made a joke about the hole in my neck. And for my wife, this is exceptionally good news.

On the blackboard, upside down and backwards, I write: *WHAT DO YOU THINK?*

'Good idea,' Jane says.

On the blackboard again, I write: *I WANT A MILLION BUCKS FOR IT!*

And now Jane is smiling, too, because this sounds like the old Evan Hunter she knows.

Before she leaves that day, she tells me Dina looks beautiful.

'She's doing it for you,' she whispers. 'And I love her for it.'

I WANTED MY HUSBAND TO wake up each morning to a cheerful, well-rested wife. I wanted to dress beautifully for him. I wanted him to find a bright smile on my face. I wanted to bring sunshine into this room each and every day we had to spend here.

I wanted him to recover.

I'M NOT SURE I ENJOY the visitors who come to see me every day.

For Dina's sake, I'm glad they're here. She's alone with me otherwise, day and night, and I know my constant coughing and spitting and complaining cannot be pleasant for her. I am not comfortable here. This is a hospital. I have just undergone serious surgery. I cannot speak. But Dina is instantly alert to my every need. In the middle of the night, the slightest stirring from me will bring her rushing to my bed from her own bed across the room. I sometimes wonder if she sleeps at all.

I cannot call for her, so we have arranged for me to knock on the adjustable bedside stand if I need her. I cannot easily reach for things because my head and neck have been wounded, and I cannot easily turn to find whatever it is I'm looking for. So I knock on that bedside stand – often knocking things to the floor in the process – and she comes to hand me the bedpan, or the gauze into which I spit my mucus, or the gadget that releases morphine into the epidural catheter at the base of my spine. And whenever a light flashes or a warning beep sounds to signal anything unusual or amiss, she runs down the hall to summon a nurse for help.

She is there for me day and night, as she's been there for me from the very moment we met.

So here we are.

But I know that the visitors brighten her day. Their unannounced arrivals are pleasant surprises that assure her of continued support and concern. She is a superb hostess, my wife, and she welcomes each new guest to our spacious hospital room – it is, after all, *Pavarotti's* Room! – as if she were greeting them at the doorway to our own home, making them comfortable, offering them food or drink, very often the fruit, candy or Starbucks cappuccino they themselves have innocently and unknowingly brought as gifts; I cannot allow anything liquid or solid to move from my mouth past those stitches holding my throat together.

When visitors arrive, there is an almost social air in that hospital room. Jokes are told, pleasantries exchanged, but although I try my best to stay with it, to remain one of the crowd, I tire easily, and often we must draw the curtain around my bed so that our friends can continue without me.

Behind the curtain, I listen to the voices talking.

I listen to the laughter of our friends.

THERE ARE FLOWERS ALL AROUND Evan's bed, everywhere in the room.

And laughter.

And love.

At a time when such tremendous change is happening in our lives, the concern of our friends helps keep me grounded. Their presence reassures me that our lives will not be that different. These people so precious to us will continue to bring love into our lives.

That will never change.

LYING BEHIND A CURTAIN, FLAT on my back in a hospital room, with a tube in my nose and another one in my throat, I wonder about many things.

When you can't speak, you have a lot of time to think.

No small talk to clutter up the sidewalk.

What I find myself thinking about these days is the immediate future.

I am beginning to wonder what life outside the safe and sterile confines of a hospital will be like for a man without a voice in a world of speaking people. In two or three days, four days, whenever they take this damn tube out of my nose and I can eat real food again, I will be released from this bed, this room, this place. What will it be like for me on the outside?

Every time I cough to spit up mucus, my daughter Amanda unwittingly reminds me that I am ... well ... different. What she does ...

Well, she simply gets up and runs out of the room.

I try to explain that this mucus is not the infected green and yellow slime accompanying a severe chest cold, it is merely the clear viscous lining that coats every passageway in the human body, and I am coughing it up because I breathe through my neck now, you see, and it is impossible for me to merely clear my throat and swallow it, the way people with larynxes do. She tells me, 'I'm sorry, Dad, I'm just squeamish,' but this does not stop her from bolting from the room every time I cough, making me feel, if not sick, then certainly ... well ... different.

But you see, my darling daughter, I will always breathe through my neck. That will never change.

I will always be coughing, even though I don't have a cold.

I am – and will continue to be – different from most other people.

I lie here and wonder a lot about this.

AT 6:00 A.M. ON THE morning of my eighth day in the hospital – I make a sound.

What?

What!

Mind you, this is not the sound of me rapping on the bedside stand for attention, nor is this the hacking sound of my coughing, oh no. This is me making a bona fide *sound* that comes from my mouth loud and clear.

The nurse just coming on does not appear startled.

Do you know that scene in the horror movie where the dead body suddenly twitches a finger and the guy in the room with him leaps for the ceiling?

Well, I was the corpse twitching a finger, and I was also that guy in the room with him. I looked around suspiciously. Scarcely daring to breathe through the hole in my neck, I tried the sound again.

Yep.

No mistake about it.

I looked at the nurse.

She went blithely about her business.

Hey, I thought. Man with no larynx just made a *sound*, why aren't you impressed?

I tried it again.

This time the nurse looked at me.

'You okay, honey?' she asked.

She had *heard* me!

I hadn't imagined it!

Oh, *yes*, I was okay! I was quite more than okay, thank you! I was well on the way to delivering the Gettysburg Address!

My first thought was: *They made a mistake.*

Oh, they removed my larynx, all right, there was no question about that, but they were wrong about that organ's speech-producing capability. Because although admittedly I had no larynx – I mean, what do you think this is, *denial* or something? I have no larynx. I know that. But I just made a sound, didn't I? The nurse heard it. She asked me if I was okay, honey. She heard the sound I made. So somebody on this fine medical staff here at this fine hospital in this fine city of New York has made a terrible mistake in believing I can no longer produce sound, I can no longer speak. I just made a sound, ergo in no time at all I will be filibustering the congress.

The sound I made is difficult to reproduce in print.

You have seen it in a lot of comic-strip balloons.

Do you know when a cartoon character says, 'Maude, that old car just quit on me?'

And Maude replies, 'Tsk, tsk, Clyde, what a shame?'

Do you know that word?

Tsk?

It isn't even a word, really, it's merely a sound.

Merely a sound?

Merely?

Merely a sound I myself made!

And it isn't pronounced 'Tisk.'

Try it. Click your tongue on the roof of your mouth. The sound you make sort of rhymes with 'itch'. It's the sound of universal sympathy. Make that sound, and you are saying, 'Oh, what a shame. Oh, what a pity.' Tsk, tsk, tsk. Titch, titch, titch. My, my, my.

I keep making the sound over and over again.

Tsk, tsk, tsk.

Dina is asleep across the room, my dear, darling wife.

I cannot wait to tell her the good news.

SUNLIGHT BREAKS THROUGH THE NORTHEAST corner of the room.

Dina stirs.

I wait until she is fully awake. Smiling, she comes to the

142

bed and kisses me on the cheek. I hold up a finger for attention. I give her a sly look. She waits expectantly.

I click my tongue against the roof of my mouth.

Tsk, tsk, tsk.

Her eyes widen in surprise.

I make the sound again.

She nods slowly.

'When did you discover this?' she asks.

I tap my wristwatch. Point to the numeral six.

'We must ask the doctors,' she says.

I answer *Tsk*, and nod.

We are developing a code.

One *tsk* is yes.

Two *tsks* are no.

And three *tsks* . . .

Ahhhh.

ON MY BLACKBOARD, I WRITE: *I CAN MAKE A SOUND.*

I write this upside down and backwards.

I CAN MAKE A SOUND.

'What do you mean?' Blaugrund asks.

'Let's hear it,' Slavit says.

I write: *IS THERE ANY WAY IT CAN HARM MY THROAT?*

This isn't really what I'm asking them. Dina knows what I'm asking. I want to know if it's possible that I'll be able to speak again. Even without a larynx, is it possible that I'll be able to make *this* sound, and then *another* sound, and eventually many *more* sounds? Is it possible that I will be able to produce human speech again?

I'm not talking about speech with a mechanical device like the one Connie Kokkalakis demonstrated for us several weeks ago. I'm not talking about esophogeal speech, either, the so-called Belch Talk kids use to dismay and disgust their

143

moms. Nor do I mean the sound generated by a prosthesis embedded in my esophagus. All of these have already been explained to me as possibilities. I am talking about *real* speech, produced by me, myself, and I. Is it at all possible that even without a larynx, I can tsk-tsk my way to normal, natural speech?

I know this simple sound can't possibly hurt my throat. I have tried it in the empty hours of the night while Dina dozed, I have tried it for her over and again this morning, waiting for the doctors to arrive on their rounds. For all this effort, my throat feels none the worse for wear. So I know that making this sound is perfectly harmless. But is it a harbinger of speech?

'Well, try it,' the anesthesiologist says.

I go *Tsk*.

I go *Tsk* again.

I keep making the sound.

Tsk. Tsk. Tsk.

'That's normal,' Blaugrund says.

'It can't hurt you,' the anesthesiologist says.

On the blackboard, I write: **BUT IT'S NOT SPEECH**.

'No,' Slavit says somewhat sorrowfully. 'It's not speech.'

'I KNOW CONNIE'S ALREADY EXPLAINED this to you,' the speech pathologist says, 'but before you leave the hospital, you should understand all the options open to you.'

Before I leave the hospital!

This is turning into a good day.

This morning, the Doctors Three *also* informed me that the stitches in my nose, and the feeding tube itself will be removed sometime later today. This means that I will soon begin eating. Food – or rather just liquids at first – will be ingested through my mouth and will move down my healing throat, into my esophagus and down into my stomach. I will be going home soon.

The pathologist is here to tell Dina and me what to expect when I get home – speechwise, that is.

Her name is Tamar, and like every speech pathologist I've met since I was diagnosed with cancer, she tends to yell when she speaks. Perhaps she is overcompensating for the fact that I cannot speak at all. Perhaps she believes removal of my larynx has also affected my hearing. In any case, she is talking too loud as she explains 'esophageal speech' to us, and I am wincing as much at the volume as at the very concept.

When I was a kid, every time I belched my mother would roll her eyes and murmur, 'Ex-*cuse* the pig.'

So I have to tell you, 'Speech by Belch' doesn't sound too terrifically appealing to me. I can see that Dina isn't enchanted by it, either. The way Tamar explains it to us, the laryngectomee (me, presumably) inhales air into his upper esophagus to produce a belch-like sound that can then be used for speech. Now, doesn't that sound delightful?

'Why does my husband have to learn that?' Dina asks.

She sounds appalled.

'As an alternate method of speech,' Tamar says.

On my blackboard, I write: **WHY?**

'In case you're not a candidate for a prosthesis.'

This does not sound like good news.

The most appealing of all the speech options discussed before I had my larynx removed was the insertion of a prosthesis in my throat. As it is re-explained now, this first requires a surgical technique known as a tracheoesophageal (phew!) puncture, shorthanded as TEP and translated as 'a hole connecting the windpipe to the food tube' – the trachea to the esophagus. Three or four days after surgery, the voice prosthesis is inserted into the puncture, and fluent conversational speech is more or less immediate.

Wow!

The prosthesis itself is a tiny hollow silicone tube that looks like a collar button, with a one-way valve at its narrow end. When its wider end is compressed, the tube can be pushed through the TEP from the trachea side, after which it regains its shape on the esophagus side and stays firmly in place. The prosthesis serves three purposes. It keeps the puncture from closing – the body seeks to close a wound, remember? It prevents leakage from the esophagus to the trachea. And – most importantly – it produces speech.

How does it produce speech?

You may well ask.

I will tell you how it produces speech.

First you take a breath.

(Much the same way you take a breath if you have a larynx and are speaking normally.)

You cover the hole in your throat with your thumb.

(Or with a little valve that can be opened or shut over the hole.)

You exhale.

(Just the way you do if you have a larynx.)

Air passes through the prosthesis and vibrates tissues in the esophagus. This creates sound.

To shape this sound into words, you use your mouth and your lips and your tongue, the same as anyone else does.

SO, WHAT'S THE CATCH? I write.

The catch is that a candidate for a prosthesis must meet certain criteria. As these are explained to me:

1. The stoma in my throat must be of sufficient size to accommodate the prosthesis – at least 1.5 cm, which is a bit more than half an inch.

2. The common wall between my esophagus and my trachea must be healthy.

3. I must be adequately motivated and emotionally stable.

4. I must have good eyesight and manual dexterity.

On my blackboard, I write **OKAY? SO?**

Assuming I can meet all these qualifications, I must then take what is known as an 'insufflation test'. This will necessitate the insertion of a rubber catheter in my nose (my *nose* again!) moving it down past what Tamar calls the 'PE segment . . .'

'That's the pharyngo-esophageal junction,' she explains. 'It's where the muscles that will produce sound are located.'

She then shows me a 'Before' and 'After' diagram of a throat similar to mine:

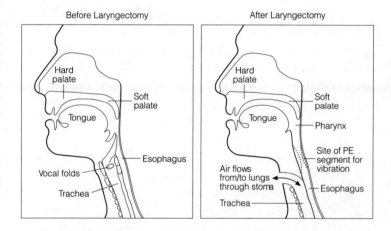

'Do you see the PE segment right here?' she asks. 'We have to test the muscles here to make certain they're capable of producing adequate sound.'

'And if they aren't capable?' Dina asks.

'Then I'm afraid your husband would not be a good candidate for a prosthesis.'

But not to worry, kiddies! There's always the so called AL, the Electronic Artificial Larynx!

And here Tamar produces just one model of the many ALs now on the market. This one is called the SERVOX®digital.

Made in Germany, its blue plastic assembly is contained in a titanium sleeve, and weighs only 5.5 ounces. At a mere 4.6 inches long by 1.3 inches in diameter, it resembles a sleek, tidy flashlight. Like a flashlight, it is powered by two rechargeable batteries. Unlike a flashlight, it does not produce illumination. Instead, it produces sound. You press a button on its side, and the device buzzes. When you hold the head of the instrument against your cheek or your throat, and simultaneously mouth silent words . . .

And here Tamar demonstrates.

'The buzz gives sound to these words.'

She does not speak these last words.

She mouths them.

The buzz gives sound to these words.

She sounds a bit like Darth Vader, but I can understand her perfectly.

'Try it,' she says.

I take the electro-larynx from her.

'Your neck may be tender,' she says. 'Try your cheek.'

I press the head of it to my right cheek.

I push the buttom.

I look at Dina and mouth the words *I love you.*

What comes out is *zzz-grr-oooo.*

'Try it again,' Tamar says. 'Move it to different places on your face. You have to find the sweet spot.'

I keep trying.

Hello, I say. *Hello. Hello. Hello.*

All I get is buzzing.

When Tamar goes off half an hour later, she leaves the electro-larynx with me, urging me to keep trying.

'It'll come to you,' she promises. 'You'll see.'

But I am convinced that unless they can put a TEP in my throat, I will never again make an intelligible sound.

*

IN MY HASTE TO COMMUNICATE now, I don't always make myself crystal clear. 'Conversation' with the nurses is completely hopeless. But even 'talking' to Dina and my daughter is difficult, often disintegrating into a virtual game of charades, with each of them guessing at the word or words I've buzzed out on my AL. As a last resort, I scribble the word or words on C.C. Wong's little blackboard.

One of the words I scribble most often is *LOGIC!*

I mean, come on kids, use your heads!

If I buzz out 'My nose hurts!' and you can't understand 'hurts', then why are you guessing 'hunts' or 'runs'? Does it look as if my nose is running? Or chasing rabbits? My nose hurts, goddamn it, *hurts*! Logic!

LOGIC!

But now my nose no longer hurts, darlings!

In three seconds flat, they remove the tube that has been tormenting me for the past eternity.

I still can't breathe through my nose, but now I don't have to eat through it, either.

Or hunt with it, either.

THERE'S A WHOLE 'NOTHER *WORLD* out there!

The doctors have been eager to get me out of bed and walking because lying flat on one's back for any extended period of time can become an invitation to pneumonia. This is my first day up, and out, and around.

But we have done this before, Dina and I.

We paraded the halls of St. Vincent's Hospital in Bridgeport after my angioplasty six years ago, and we paraded them again at Johns Hopkins in Baltimore four months after that when the angioplasty closed. Dina slept in the room at St. Vincent's, and she slept in the room at Johns Hopkins, too . . .

A nurse in the hallway there, seeing both of us strolling in

robes one morning, holding hands, said, 'Oh, how *wonderful*!
Did you meet here?'

... and she slept in the room at the Cleveland Clinic,
where one morning as we took our obligatory walk down
the hall we were stopped by Muslim guards who barred
our way because the Queen Mother of Dubai was in
residence and we were not permitted to see her unveiled
face ...

... and Dina sleeps in the room here at Lenox Hill as well.
And now, together, and holding hands, we walk another
hospital corridor yet another time, pushing our silent
'dancing partner' ahead of us.

WHEN HE IS IN BED, there are tubes hanging everywhere
around my husband. Before we can take our little corridor
strolls, we must first detach the large blue tube that carries
moisture to his lungs and hangs loosely over his stoma, its
plastic tray attached with a gauze string around his neck.
There is always something dripping into the IV tube leading
into Evan's arm, and there is yet another tube connected to
the pain-management machine. Leaving the bed requires
quite a bit of maneuvering and putting on an extra robe over
all these attachments makes the task even more challenging.
But once Evan is on his feet, our little march down the hall is
really quite simple. In fact, it's almost jaunty.

The wheeled pole supporting the several plastic bags is on
Evan's right.

He shoves it ahead of us with his right hand.

His left hand is holding mine.

BEYOND THE LUXURIOUS PRINCIPALITY OF Pavarotti's Room,
there is a cluster of other rooms in which other princes and
princesses – many of them far older and far sicker than I –

hold tenuous sway. Dina and I stroll slowly up the corridor, careful not to look into these other rooms; there is little enough privacy on a hospital floor.

We pass the nurses' station. I let go of Dina's hand only to buzz out a few words of greeting on my electro-larynx. The nurses pass the time of day with me . . .

'My, are you walking already?'

'Don't you look fine!'

'When are you taking him home, Mrs. Hunter?'

I'm still not sure I want to go home just yet.

Out there, it's a whole 'nother world all *over* again.

Out there, it's a jungle.

Dina is thinking much the same thing.

ON OUR NUMEROUS WALKS THROUGH the corridors, we begin making plans for the immediate future, and then plans for when Evan gets his prosthesis and can talk again, and then plans for beyond that. There is no doubt in our minds that within six months we will be able to resume our lives fully, begin to catch up with time lost, work left behind, travel plans cancelled. We are each other's strongest support; we do not need anyone else.

I tell this to the social worker who comes to talk to us about Evan's coming release from the hospital. She looks at me skeptically and then asks if we're experiencing any depression, are we going to need any counseling?

'No,' I tell her, 'we're fine.'

'Because, you know,' she says, 'you're the one who'll have to take care of your husband.' I look at her. 'Until he's strong enough to care for himself,' she says.

I begin to explain how I felt the first time I saw my husband's throat being suctioned.

'I could never do that,' I tell her.

151

'Well, if you can't, you can't,' she says calmly, and leaves the room.

A TUBE WAS ABOUT TO go down into Evan's lungs again.

We would be going home any day now, and I knew nothing at all about morning care, evening care, *any* care. I was not a nurse! How could I possibly help my husband? I was nothing but a peasant girl from a tiny village in Serbia. I kept asking myself, Well, what did you think? Did you think your husband's stoma would miraculously heal the moment you stepped out of the hospital? Did you think you would be worry-free forever after?

Well, yes, that was a logical presumption, wasn't it? Once we left the hospital, we would leave our problems behind as well. We had crossed many hospital thresholds together before, my husband and I, and my experience so far had lulled me into the belief that this time would be no different from any of the others. Wasn't that logical? If not, why hadn't anyone contradicted it till now?

The nurse attending Evan was wearing on her uniform a big button that read *#1 NURSE*. I figured a member of her family had given it to her; I figured they thought she was a good woman as well as a good nurse. I hoped so. She showed me a small plastic package with the words SUCTION KIT on it.

'This is all sterile,' she said. 'You have to be careful to keep it that way, so that everything that goes into the lungs or touches the wound will be absolutely clean.'

She carefully opened the package, removed from it a small paper towel coated on one side with plastic, and placed this on the counter. A box inside the package was divided into small compartments, each of them holding different tools, carefully wrapped and easily accessible. With her right hand, she pulled a plastic glove over her left. With the now-gloved left hand, she pulled a second glove over her right hand. With this hand, she opened a small plastic bottle and filled a cup with saline solution.

'My right hand is no longer sterile,' she said. 'Because I used it to open the bottle. The right hand is my dominant hand. I'm going to use it from now on to touch anything that's already been exposed. I'll keep my left hand sterile at all times.'

She removed a plastic tube from its paper sleeve. Still using the clean left hand, she connected the sterile tube that would go down Evan's throat to the sterile tube attached to the suctioning machine. Her right hand went to the stoma to remove the plastic vent that was keeping the wound open. Her left hand was holding the sterile tube, still slightly curled after being wrapped in its paper sleeve. It looked harmless. But the moment she raised the pressure and dipped the tube into sterile saline water, it uncoiled like a snake about to strike. When she slipped it into my husband's throat, I almost turned away.

But I had to learn how to do this.

I had been through many scary moments with Evan. Two heart attacks and the Triple A – by far the scariest of them all. But nothing that had gone before could compare to this. While my husband gasped for breath and helplessly flapped his hands in despair, tears streaming down his face, there was nothing I could do but watch in silence.

And learn.

When the social worker arrived the next morning to tell me she was exploring the possibility of placing my husband in a hospice somewhere, my response was firm:

'My husband is coming home with me,' I said.

*

DURING DR. SLAVIT'S VISIT BEFORE Evan's release from the hospital, I ran after him in the corridor, and asked if he'd yet received the pathology report.

'I spoke to them on the phone,' he said. 'They found cancer cells in the soft tissue.'

'Soft tissue?' I said.

'The tissue that surrounds the lymph nodes.'

As he explained that the cancer had been growing underneath the vocal cords, making it impossible to see, I thought only *How did we let this happen?* We were seeing you almost every month, Evan's voice began changing two *years* ago, how could cancer have been growing undetected all this time?

'Because of the radiation, no malignant growth showed on the surface,' Dr. Slavit explained.

But it was there, I thought, it was *there*!

I remembered reading a paragraph in Michael Korda's book, *Man to Man*. The doctors at Memorial Sloan Kettering were telling Korda that cancer was sometimes difficult to find, but if it was there, they 'were prepared to keep digging until they found it.'

So why hadn't Blaugrund and Slavit found it?

Surrounded by resident doctors now, Dr. Slavit explained that over the years, any time a doctor examining Evan had discovered a growth on his vocal cords, he'd removed it and sent it for biopsy. The results had always come back negative.

'I've been talking to Dr. Harrison at Beth Israel,' he told me. 'About possibly radiating . . .'

'But Evan's already *had* radiation . . .'

'Yes, but only his *larynx* was radiated. Very little radiation spilled out onto the surrounding tissue. Harrison thinks he may be able to radiate Evan's entire *neck* this time.'

I said nothing.

My husband still has cancer, I thought.

DIANE BERNHARD – WHO WROTE, DIRECTED, and performed *The Sound of Evan* – is the only woman I know who has her own chauffered limo. She once told a gay chauffeur, 'The only queen in this limo is *me!*' When she offers the limo to us for our trip home from the hospital, Dina and I accept her generosity without hesitation.

I am dressed and ready to leave at eight on Saturday morning, 10 August.

This is the first time I'm wearing street clothes since 30 July, eleven days ago. I feel like a different person. Maybe that's because I'm now a person with a nostril in my throat.

One by one, the nurses come by to say their farewells.

We hug.

We kiss each other on the cheek.

I promise to send them signed books.

Diane's chauffeur – Polish this time, and not gay – carries down the supplies that will see us through the days and weeks ahead, and then he comes back upstairs to fetch us. A nurse's aide has brought a wheelchair for me. We stop at the nurses' station one last time, and I reach up out of the chair for my final hugs and kisses.

I am scared as hell.

But on the way down to the waiting limo, Diane's chauffeur accompanying us, the nurse's aide pushing the chair from behind, Dina by my side, I know that never again will I allow anyone to leave me in a noisy corridor facing a blank wall.

We are heading home.

5

HOME, SWEET HOME

COMING HOME HAD NEVER BEEN so sweet, our lawn never so green, our rose blooms never so abundant as on that sunny day of August tenth, when the Bernhard limo slowly pulled into our driveway and took us to the front door of the house. As Evan and I stepped out of the car, country breezes bid us a warm, sweet welcome. The murmur of the river reached to us. There were birds everywhere, seeming to chirp only for us. We smiled at each other. With his electro-larynx, Evan said, 'Let's enjoy all this, honey,' and took my hand, and together we entered the house.

We were home at last.

That night, for the first time in thirteen days, Evan and I fell asleep in our own house, in our own bed, in each others' arms.

12 AUGUST IS A BLISTERING hot day.

The visiting nurse tells us at once that as soon as she's finished here this morning, she's going home to dunk in her pool. In the next ten minutes, Dina and I learn that she is the office supervisor and doesn't usually go out in the field. We also learn that she hasn't dealt with a laryngectomy patient in at least ten years. In fact, this is the first time she's ever even *seen* a Nebulizer.

'We'll learn how to use it together,' she says, smiling pleasantly.

For some reason, I find this somewhat less than reassuring.

She takes my temperature and my blood pressure.

Everything is normal. I have no larynx, but otherwise everything is normal. Together, she and Dina read the instructions that came in the box with the Nebulizer.

'Let's see now,' the nurse says. 'I think this goes here . . . and this goes there . . .'

An hour later, she has still not figured out how to put it together, so she makes a call to the medical supply company to ask that they send a technician out as soon as possible.

This is not a life-threatening situation, you understand. I am simply waiting for a Mucomyst treatment that will start me coughing again. (In fact, I am secretly pleased that the ordeal will be postponed until the man from the medical supply company can get here to help us assemble this dread machine.) Meanwhile, the nurse smiles pleasantly, bids us a fond *adieu*, and promises to see us again tomorrow morning at nine. For her, it's off to the pool!

For us, it's growing accustomed to a vast house gone suddenly still.

MAKING EVAN COMFORTABLE IS A PRIORITY.

We have settled him in the upstairs bedroom, a large, sunny room open to the garden. I've brought in extra pillows, so that he can sit up in bed, which facilitates coughing. A long, wooden desk below the windows and off to the side of the bed is a perfect place to put the supplies we brought home from the hospital.

On this table, close to the bed, I also place the humidifier, a small machine fitted with a pressure scale and a small nozzle to which a plastic bottle is attached. I fill the bottle with sterile water, and attach the now-familiar blue tube to it, a plastic tray at its opposite end.

I turn on the switch, and let the pressure rise to the desired intensity.

Bubbles began to form.

I watch their little dance.

The tray fills with steam, and I fasten its plastic ribbon around my husband's neck, letting it hang loose over his stoma. The familiar muted rumble of the machine and the soft hiss of the bubbling water permeate the room.

OUR LARGE BATHROOM WAS ONCE two bathrooms that Evan and I changed into a single large room when we bought the house. A Jacuzzi is now framed by windows that flood the room with light. The light reflects in the mirrors above the sinks across the room. It is a bright and beautiful spot for me to set up shop.

I choose the space between the two sinks and move the Chinese wooden planter filled with orchids to the other side of the room, next to the Jacuzzi. I then place the two units of the suction machine side by side. One of these is the small motor that will produce suction; the other is simply a clear plastic container that will gather mucus.

I connect these separate halves of the machine with small, plastic tubes and pour a little water into the clear container.

I open the laryngectomy kit, careful to pinch the gloves with only two fingers of my dominant hand, careful to keep the other hand sterile at all times.

I pour saline into the small container, attach the sterile, plastic tube to the suction machine, turn the power on, and dip the plastic tube into the saline water. Before I place the suction tube in my husband's stoma each time, I will have to perform this small task to make routinely certain that everything is working properly.

Liquid from the cup rushes into the clear container with a sudden slurping sound that startles me.

I arrange my retaining trays and all the supplies I will need here on the countertop: the various kits, the extra drain sponges, the cloth ties that fasten the trach tube to Evan's neck, the long, sterile cotton Q-tips, the sterile gauze, the box of sterile gloves, the 3ml saline ampoules, the Bacitracin ointment, the bottles of peroxide, alcohol, and saline water.

I step back to look at my workspace again.

Everything seems in order.

In the bedroom, Evan is dozing.

The house is so very still.

When Evan and I bought this house, we had almost every wall knocked down, trying to give it the feeling of a loft, while keeping its country charm. We decorated our bedroom with an Italian wrought-iron bed, hand-painted Italian cabinets and a Venetian mirror. Next to an upholstered chaise longue is a tall lamp that looks like a loose bouquet of tulips, each bloom a different-colored glass blown in Murano, near Venice, where we were married. On each of the cabinets, there are vases filled with flowers from our garden. Framed pictures of our wedding stand alongside the blooms.

In the silent room, in this silent house, I smile.

This is a lovely place for my husband to recover.

I GO INTO EVAN'S LUNGS every day of the week.

Or at least, I insert a plastic suctioning tube to just where his bronchial tube branches into his lungs. From the pages the visiting nurse has photocopied for me, I learn the maximum length of tube that can be inserted before it begins to coil or twist. She teaches me how to keep the tube in one hand while guiding it with the other, lowering it into the stoma, moving it gently to remove mucus. Now that the wound is no longer heavily discharging, I learn that a softer red tube will serve the same purpose, and when I switch to that, our morning routine becomes more pleasant.

Every morning, every night, the routine takes at least two hours.

I am told it will get easier.

OUR FRIENDS COME TO VISIT, but after just a week, we can no longer find the energy to receive them. Our house, once so full of happy laughter, has now become silent.

Time moves slowly. I have no desire to share my feelings with anyone. Afraid that my husband may be able to read my pain, I begin to slip into a lonely world, turning my broken heart away from him. Silence moves in, and sadness takes hold of me. Evan keeps his distance. If he notices my presence, he moves to another remote corner of the house.

A VOICE IS COMING FROM behind the closed door of our library. Surprised, I gently open the door. Evan is sitting on the leather sofa, looking at the floor, his shoulders hunched, his elbows on his knees, his hands cradling his head. The posters of films made from his books are framed on the wall behind him. Bookshelves filled with audio tapes of every book he's written are on the wall opposite. This cozy room with its fireplace and its television screen was always our safe haven, our retreat at the end of the day.

The room is now filled with a strong, masculine voice – my husband's. But it is coming from a taped interview Evan gave to the BBC, long before his throat was invaded by cancer.

I curl up at his feet. I find my way into his embrace.

His hand gently pats my head. I begin crying in his lap.

My husband grieves his silence in silence.

WORK IS MY SALVATION.

Before I went into the hospital for surgery, I'd completed nine pages of a short story titled *Leaving Nairobi*, and thirty pages of *The Frumious Bandersnatch*, the next 87th Precinct novel.

I got out of the hospital on 10 August, and was back at my

desk on 19 August. On 22 August, I e-mailed the first of my medical reports to my family and friends:

August 22, 2002

Dear Kiddies:

First, some terminology. The (permanent) hole in my throat is called a stoma, don't ask me why. When the stoma is open, I breathe through it. When it is closed (either by my thumb or a valve later on) trapped air will be forced into my mouth through a prosthesis, and my tongue and lips will produce virtually human speech.

A TEP is a Tracheal Esophageal Puncture. Once this is made in the esophagus, a tiny silicone piece will be inserted in the puncture, and then (I guess) TEP will stand for Tracheal Esophageal *Prosthesis*. Trapped air is forced through the prosthesis, causing it to vibrate and etc as above, to produce speech.

All clear?

Today, I went to see the doctor. Everything is healing properly. He opted not to remove the stitches around the stoma (See? There's your new word!) today because on September 4 – hooray! – he will perform the TEP and insert the TEP, and he will remove the stitches at that time, when I won't feel tugging or pulling or any pain.

The TEP procedure will take one hour under general anesthesia. Another hour in the recovery room. The speech pathologist will come to see me immediately afterward to show me how to place my thumb on the stoma to use my new device. I'll be in my own home, and talking again that very afternoon. Probably just counting from one to ten and back again, but hey, speech is speech and I'm not running for president.

We learned today, that most 'laryngectomees' (the group name for those of us who have had our larynxes removed) undergo radiation therapy afterward as insurance against any rampant cells that may still be lurking. Although a CAT scan and a later PET scan both revealed no cancer anywhere else in my body, my doctor feels that if radiation will do no harm, it is to be advised. We will be meeting with a radiologist shortly after Labor Day, and the decision will be made at that time. I rather suspect radiation will be recommended. If so, it will mean five days a week for six weeks. After that, all the tissue in my throat should be sterile, and I can sing again at the Met with no fears.

So that's it.

Dina and I are considerably up after talking to both my doctor and the speech pathologist today. We'll be going into New York again next week to get a preview of how my new voice will sound, and then it'll be September 4 before you know it!

That's it for today. I hope this isn't more than you cared to know. I'll continue to keep you informed if you like.

Much love,

Evan

IN THE HOSPITAL, EVAN WORE a metal trach tube in his throat day in and day out. This 'trake' tube was ordered by Dr. Blaugrund, after the laryngectomy, and it was made to measure, especially to fit Evan's stoma and trachea. Sitting solidly inside the stoma, its weight and rigidity prevented it from moving too much. This was very important to the healing process; movement might have irritated and possibly damaged the healing stoma.

The elbow-shaped tube resembles nothing more than a small piece of shiny plumbing. Constructed of unforgiving metal, the outer sleeve has a smaller metal tube within, which I remove for cleaning every morning and evening, and often during the day as well, whenever excessive mucus gathers.

For more than two weeks now, this tube has been sticking in my husband's throat day and night.

He has begun to think of it as a medieval instrument of torture.

I EAT LIKE A BABY.

Everything I eat comes from a jar with a picture of the Gerber baby on it, or else has been pulverized in a blender until it becomes pap. I can smell nothing. But I can still taste food, which is something of a surprise.

I cough incessantly.

I was told at MEETH that the coughing and clearing of mucus would get better as time went by. (They were smart enough not to tell me I'd 'get used to it'.) Instead, they said it would gradually improve until I'd be coughing maybe four or five times a day. Well, this is not true as yet. I cough all day long, I bring up mucus all day long. Some days are worse than others, but *every* day is a bad day. I cough all day long, clearing mucus interminably, sometimes almost choking on it.

I have no larynx, you see.

THE METAL TUBE IN MY husband's throat is there to keep the stoma open while it heals. As I understand this, as long as tissue keeps dividing to heal a wound, the body will try to compensate for whatever was taken away from it by restoring the wound to its original state. In short, the body will keep trying to close the hole in my husband's throat. And if that happens, he will be unable to breathe.

Drs. Blaugrund and Slavit gave my husband a perfect stoma: large, entirely round, with hardly any scar tissue at all, it is a perfect circle through which I can easily see the soft pink tissue of Evan's windpipe descending to his lungs, a privileged intimacy that never fails to fill me with tenderness. But a large, open stoma also means that I can reach into it easily with my surgical tweezers, to pluck out dried mucus; it means that Evan can cough out debris, keeping his lungs clear. And it means that a voice prosthesis can later be easily installed and maintained.

It means that my husband will one day speak again.

MEANWHILE, I'VE STARTED HICCUPING.

Yep.

I am certain this is caused by the laryngectomy, but Slavit assures me it has nothing to do with it. I feel like Pope Pius XII, who – deceived by a charlatan posing as a medical doctor – was prescribed treatment that gave the Holy Father chronic hiccups and rotting teeth.

I hiccup day and night.

This is not hyperbole.

I hiccup every thirty seconds, day or night.

Is *Slavit* himself a charlatan?

Will *my* teeth turn rotten?

Then what?

I AM ALSO AFRAID OF going into the shower.

I am afraid I will drown in the shower.

I have been told I will never swim again because if water enters that hole in my throat it will go directly to the lungs, and I will drown. Okay, so no more swimming. But what's to prevent water in the shower from entering that same hole and causing a similar untimely demise?

One of the items of self-preservation recommended by the visiting hospital social worker was a device called a Shower-Shield, which is a protective collar that fits around the neck with a Velcro fastener. Made of soft, pliable vinyl, it is easy to put on, and easy to take off. It covers the stoma completely, and allows breathing through a sort of scooped out channel at the bottom. Not only do I fasten this to my neck every morning, but Dina sticks paper adhesive tape to its edges where it joins the neck, just to make sure no water seeps in around it, and finds its way to the stoma, and drowns me.

Even so, I am in and out of that shower in two minutes flat. Who wants to drown just breathing?

FOR A LARYNGECTOMEE, BREATHING AND talking are two quite different things. Breathing comes naturally. Instead of using your nose or your mouth – you can't use them anymore, anyway; your larynx is gone – you simply take in air through the hole in your throat. You don't have to think about this. You breathe quite naturally, the same way you always did, but the air is now coming in through the hole in your throat. It's as simple as . . . well . . . breathing.

In fact, nothing about breathing has really changed except that the hairs in your nostrils no longer filter the air you breathe, and the air is no longer warmed and moistened by its passage through the nose and throat, which means that cold, polluted, or simply dry air goes straight down into your lungs. This causes coughing. Coughing brings up mucus. This is what you do all day long. You cough and you bring up mucus.

As for talking . . .

For now, you use the electro-larynx.

It takes some getting used to, this little buzzing apparatus.

Even though my throat is still healing, I've been practicing in front of the mirror and I have now located the so-called sweet spot where the instrument fits snugly against the skin and no buzzing escapes from around it. I'm left-handed, so this is on the left side of my neck. Also, by pressing softer or harder against the skin, I've learned how to produce a better 'voice'. I can now locate the sweet spot without having to stand in front of a mirror. Over and over again, I've practiced making the most difficult sounds – p, t, k, s, f, ch, sh, and th – and using them at the beginning of words.

I am not reluctant to use the electro-larynx in the presence of friends, who tell me they can understand me completely – especially on the phone, where the frequency of the instrument seems to transmit itself quite clearly. But Dina and I haven't ventured out to a restaurant yet.

That will come later.

We hope.

I CANNOT STOP HICCUPING.

I try all the tricks I know. I hold my breath. Just when I think I've succeeded, I hiccup again. I put a forefinger in each ear, and without taking a breath, I swallow a glass of water Dina holds for me. On a visit to the city, Slavit tells me everything will be all right, I'll get used to it.

I tell him I cannot swallow food.

He advises me to eat softer food.

I tell him that every time I try to swallow softer food, I hiccup.

I tell him I am ready to slit my throat.

But they've already done that.

WHILE DR. SLAVIT'S NURSE WAS writing a new prescription for the Mucomyst medication, I happened to ask if she could also give me some new syringes, as I'd run out of them.

She handed me some samples she kept in a drawer, and then explained the proper proportion in which to mix them: one unit of medication to three units of saline water.

I looked at the syringes.

They seemed so small.

Much smaller than the ones I was using at home.

MEA CULPA.

I was overdosing my husband on Mucomyst!

The syringes I'd been given by the visiting nurse had come with no instructions. She hadn't asked me if I knew how to read the measurements on them, nor did I know enough to realize I might be doing something wrong. She simply presumed I would know what to do, and I presumed likewise.

The very next day, I gave Evan just a third of the Mucomyst dosage.

The hiccups eased at first in intensity, then in frequency, and finally disappeared entirely.

When I found the courage to tell him that I was the one who'd caused them, he opened his eyes wide in exaggerated shock, and produced a huge fake hiccup. Then he made the sign of the cross on the air, and grinned, and placed his hand on my head in papal forgiveness.

BY THE END OF THAT week, I'd finished *Leaving Nairobi*.

By the end of the month, just before I went into the hospital again to have the TEP performed, *Bandersnatch* was on page seventy. I had been home for three weeks. I had agreed to a new contract with S&S, and I was looking forward to speaking again soon.

THE INSPECTOR GENERAL ARRIVES AT the stroke of nine on 30 August, a month to the day after I had my larynx removed. She has come down from the Office of the Visiting Nurse Service, and she is there to tell us that we no longer qualify for home care. She is a mousy little woman who reminds me of a secretary I once had (and fired), and she explains that since we now know how to use the various machines and are capable of self-medication without assistance, we no longer need a nurse coming by every morning. We agree that we no longer need a nurse. But we *do* need supplies. We use supplies at an alarming rate, and supplies cost money, and as long as we are still eligible for home care, Medicare should pay for those supplies.

The Inspector General does not agree.

She gives me an unsolicited lecture on the level of poverty in the state of Connecticut, and the plight of those poor unfortunates living in Bridgeport – 'You should *see* some of the homes I go into' – and how someone 'as obviously well-off' as I am (a roll of the eyes here to indicate our luxurious surroundings) should be able to pay for his own supplies.

It is difficult to get angry when you're using an electro-larynx. But I hold the instrument to the sweet spot on my cheek, and I tell her as clearly and as distinctly as I can that I've been working since I was fifteen years old when I started delivering groceries over the summer so that I could afford a senior-prom tuxedo and flowers for my girl, and I've been contributing 1.45% of my income to Medicare ever since 1941, and am now *entitled* to whatever benefits my government is obliged to give me after a serious illness.

*So please don't go telling me how well-*off *I am*! I buzz like an angry bee. *It's none of your damn business how well-*off *I am!*

She sits there stony-faced.

I am staring at a blank wall again.

'I'm taking you off home care,' she says. 'If you'll sign this, please?'

What is it?

'A release saying you agree you no longer need assistance.'

I won't sign it.

'You don't have to. I'm taking you off home care, anyway.'

And she storms out in a huff.

And the house goes silent again.

THE DAY WE WENT TO see Dr. Slavit about installing Evan's indwelling prosthesis, we sat in his waiting room opposite a man who'd also had a laryngectomy. Evan quickly brought his electro-larynx to his neck to wish him good morning. No reply, not even an effort, just an angry rumble. Evan took my hand. The man sat with his back turned to his beautiful wife, alone in their separate pain. She managed to give us a weak smile, but she remained silent beside her husband, who never once looked at her.

I felt glad I was not that woman.

BEFORE WE LEFT HIS OFFICE that day, Dr. Slavit handed me a sealed envelope containing a copy of Evan's pathology report.

MICROSCOPIC DIAGNOSIS:

Transglottic squamous cell carcinoma, moderately differentiated, involving midline, laryngeal ventricle and true and false vocal cords on the left, and extending into aryepiglottic fold and pyriform sinus on the left.

Excision margins of left pharynx/base of tongue, positive (slide L)

Midline aryepiglottic tissue, positive 0.3cm from inked margin (slide AF)

Lymphatic invasion present.

Thyroid ossified cartilage invaded by tumor (slide W, AB, AC)

Tracheal, skeletal muscle and thyroid margins, negative.

DR. SLAVIT HAD EARLIER INFORMED me that the cancer had invaded Evan's soft tissues, but now – although I could not understand all of the medical language – there were words in the pathology report that disturbed me.

*Excision margins . . . **positive**.*
*Lymphatic **invasion present**.*
*Thyroid cartilage **invaded by tumor**.*

I DON'T KNOW WHY I never looked at that report. I guess I was confident that radiation would take care of any cancer that still remained in my body. It was only months later that my internist translated it into plain English for Dina and me:

A malignant tumor of the larynx, involving both vocal cords and extending into the surrounding tissue with invasion of the thyroid cartilage and lymph channels.

DR. LOUIS B. HARRISON, CHAIRMAN of Radiation Oncology at Beth Israel Medical Center, is a man in his early fifties, I guess, about five-feet-nine, trim and dapper in tan slacks, a lime green button-down shirt, and a matching green-and-tan striped tie. This is the third day of September, and tomorrow morning Dr. Slavit will perform the minor procedure that will create a passage from my trachea to my esophagus, allowing the insertion of a prosthesis that will enable me to talk again.

Harrison examines my throat visually and with instruments, feels my neck with both hands, and tells me it will be perfectly all right for me to begin radiation therapy as soon as I've recovered from the tracheoesophageal (phew!) procedure scheduled for tomorrow.

He then explains why he and Dr. Slavit both feel I will benefit greatly from such radiation. They had both read the pathology report.

As he now translates this for us, there is no evidence of cancer in my neck. None. Zip. A CAT Scan and a PET Scan both revealed no cancer anywhere *else* in my body, either. However, the cancer *had* spread to the cartilage in my neck (the

173

Adam's apple) and had entered the lymphatic channel. Cartilage and channel have already been removed, and what remains is presumably healthy tissue.

But . . .

(In Medland, there is always a 'but . . .')

'This was a very extensive cancer,' he says.

So . . .

On the off chance that an outlaw cell or cells may have escaped into the lymph nodes themselves, it is thought wise to radiate the rest of my neck to destroy anything nasty that may be lingering. As Blaugrund once put it, 'You can never turn your back on cancer.' I believed him then. I believe Harrison now.

But Dina looks him dead in the eye.

'This is a frightening report, isn't it?' she asks.

'Yes, it is,' he answers.

'How could this have happened?' she says. 'We saw Dr. Slavit every month!'

'I wasn't there then,' Harrison replies. 'I'm here now.'

I look at him. I look at Dina.

'Do I positively *need* this radiation?' I ask.

'Yes,' Harrison replies. 'You positively *need* it.'

He once worked with Ghossein ('Forgive me, I'm very fussy!') which would be reason enough to choose him as the radiologist who will be in charge of my treatments. But when I ask him why I should shlep into New York City five days a week, instead of going to any one of the many radiologists in Connecticut, he says, modestly, 'Because I'm the best there is.'

And that's good enough for me.

WE WALK CROSSTOWN AND THROUGH Stuyvesant Park, the very patch of greenery Dina and I traversed five summers ago, when occasionally she would accompany me to my mid-morning radiation treatments. Back then, after Ghossein zapped me, we would go to a little Italian restaurant (have you noticed that people always refer to Italian restaurants as 'little' Italian restaurants, I wonder why) where we would have a simple lunch and discuss our future together.

The future is now.

It is a bright sunny day at the beginning of September. Tonight, we will sleep at the Lotos Club on East 66th Street, here in New York, and early tomorrow morning we will walk over to Manhattan Eye, Ear, Nose and Throat on East 64th, where another long corridor leading to another Operating Room will beckon. Meanwhile, we stroll in dappled sunshine, my wife and I, on our way to Beth Israel's Petrie Division on 16th Street and First Avenue, where Harrison has made an appointment for us to see Dr. Joshua Verona, an attendant dentist in the hospital's Otolaryngology Department.

Verona turns out to be a tall slender man who tells me he, too, was born and raised in New York City. We reminisce about the good old days – my good old days are a lot older than his – and then he examines my mouth and tells me the left second lower molar and the right first lower molar may pose threats in the future and should be extracted.

The news is somewhat difficult to accept. Why should two perfectly healthy teeth have to be extracted? Well, because when the neck is radiated, the lower jaw may be affected, and if there is ever any problem with the teeth in the future, any radiated tissue will cause serious complications. Scatter radiation, as it is called, may permanently close off the blood vessels, making healing impossible.

So . . .

Since teeth eighteen and thirty appear to be a trifle 'mobile', and therefore 'periodontally compromised', as we say in the trade, they will have to go.

In Medland, they give you information morsel by morsel.

There is always 'Other News' in Medland. First they tell you your larynx must go. Next they tell you your throat has to be radiated. Then they tell you two teeth have to be extracted before you can begin radiation. When will they tell you they have to cut off your balls? Or have they already?

But hark, there is yet more!

Verona now takes molds of my upper and lower teeth so that he can have trays made that will fit snugly over the teeth as I perform my obligatory evening ablutions. Into these trays, I will squeeze a fluoride solution that will remain in the trays and in my mouth for five minutes every night, before I go to bed. What is the purpose of this ritual? To protect my teeth from infection. Because if my teeth become infected, and need treatment, then the radiated tisue may da-dah da-dah da-dah.

But, pray, Dr. Verona, how long must I go on putting these fluoride-loaded trays into my mouth each night?

'Forever,' sayeth the good doctor.

Forever.

You are still in Medland, kiddo.

TEP.

Tracheoesophageal (gasp!) puncture.

Actually, the procedure was far simpler than its pronunciation. Under general anesthesia, Slavit and his team (no Blaugrund this time) poked through the trachea into the esophagus, and then passed that little silicone prosthesis into my mouth, down my throat, and finally through the fresh puncture. Once the prosthesis was properly positioned, Slavit removed the guide wire, and I was reversed from general anesthesia. An hour after it had all begun, I was in the Recovery Room, in stable condition, and breathing on my own.

*

AT THE RECEPTIONIST'S DESK IN the Recovery Room, there was an endless argument between the nurse in charge and the driver of an elderly woman who was unable to answer questions about her hospital bills. They were now trying to reach her daughter by phone, somewhere in the United States. Evan was sitting in a chair, dressed in street clothes now, ready to hear his new voice.

Connie asked him what his address was.

I closed my eyes and listened to him speak first the number, and then the name of our street, and the name of our little town, Weston, and then the state, Connecticut. Then tears came. Tears of sorrow, yes, because in that instant we were bidding goodbye to all we had lost forever. But tears of joy as well; Evan was speaking.

My husband saw the tears.

He took my hand.

'I love you,' he said.

I HAVE SINCE HEARD OTHER laryngectomees speaking for the first time.

They will always turn to their partners or their spouses, and the first words they invariably speak are 'I love you'.

The words come out shakily at first, in a voice that is certainly not your own, but which somehow has the same inflection your natural voice had, the same nuances, yes, you can hear yourself, this is you, yes, and you are speaking.

I counted from one to ten, I recited the alphabet, my voice – this odd new voice that was now mine – growing stronger with each passing moment.

And at last, when they told me I could go now, I stood up and took Dina's hand in my own, and in a booming, joyful, exuberant voice I'm sure they heard all the way in Brooklyn I shouted, 'Okay, Toots, let's go!'

Dina burst out laughing.

We were on our way again.

September 5, 2002

Well, yesterday they inserted the voice prosthesis.

The voice sounds sort of gurgly on this first day, but that will clear up. Otherwise, it's a good strong voice, quite unlike what my natural voice sounded like. More McBain than Hunter, if you will. You can judge for yourself in due course. You'll probably hear it within the next two weeks or so, as soon as I've mastered how to produce it.

We spoke to the radiologist at Beth Israel on Tuesday. He, too, agrees that radiation is advisable. So I'll be trotting in to Beth Israel for six weeks, five days a week, starting on the sixteenth. Better safe than sorry.

We don't know how we'll manage this yet. It should not be an insurmountable journey. Some guys make the trip every day, commuting to their jobs. We're hoping we can schedule afternoon treatments, so that I can work all morning, have lunch here, commute to New York, and then take an express train back, to be home in time for dinner. We'll see how it works out.

That's it for now. Talk to you soon (literally!)

I COULD NOT UNDERSTAND HOW such a simple procedure could cause such agonizing pain afterward.

I complained to Slavit that the prosthesis and the metal trach tube seemed incompatible. He told me, Yes, I needed a plastic tube with a hole in it, like the one Connie has already ordered.

I told him that even when the tube was out of my throat, I found it hard to swallow. 'It feels as if food is catching on the prosthesis,' I said.

He told me this probably had only to do with the swelling after the TEP surgery.

I told him I was belching constantly, and that I had the

constant feeling I was about to throw up. He said that was probably due to the difficulty I was having swallowing, and the fact that I was swallowing a lot of air.

I told him, Yes, but I actually *do* throw up after meals!

He said, 'Eat a little less at each meal.'

I told him I felt as if I were trying to dislodge the prosthesis, belch it up or cough it up, as if there were something in my throat that didn't *want* to be there. I told him I was afraid to leave the trach tube out for fear the hole would close in and we'd have to do the operation all over again, but the tube was so unyielding that it seemed to be *fighting* the prosthesis.

He suggested that I come into the city tomorrow afternoon sometime so that Connie could insert the softer tube.

I told him, 'No, I don't want to wait till tomorrow afternoon sometime, there is too much pain and discomfort, I want to come in *today* sometime, *now*!'

He told me he would call Connie to see if the new tube had arrived.

ON 8 SEPTEMBER, A YEAR ago, I was in Bryn Mawr, Pennsylvania, where I'd just started the book tour for *Money, Money, Money*. I drove home after the signing so that I could spend our fourth wedding anniversary at home with my wife. Now 9/9/97 had magically become 9/9/02, and we were still together, despite the pundits who had prophesied, 'I give it a month.'

Last 9 September, I'd ordered champagne for all the other diners in the restaurant – not such a big deal since there were only ten or twelve of them. This 9 September, before we went out, I removed the soft plastic tube I was wearing, and covered the hole in my throat with a stoma cover. The prosthesis no longer caused pain, and since I was now able to swallow again, Dina and I went back to the same small French restaurant in Southport, and dined alone, and renewed our vows.

I could no longer drink champagne or any other alcoholic beverage. Since I'd been taught that it was bad luck to make a toast with a non-alcoholic drink, we simply clasped hands and told each other that things were getting better all the time, and that soon this would all be behind us.

I REMEMBER THAT I ORDERED the *fois gras* and the duck, and Evan ordered the *escargot* and the fish. For dessert, I had the *soufflé* and Evan his favorite chocolate *coullant*. We were in a celebratory mood, and happy.

When we returned home, suddenly, without warning, my husband of five years began throwing up all the food he'd eaten that night.

We cleaned the sink. We were not panicked. But when we tried to reinsert the size-twelve tube, we discovered that in a scant few hours, Evan's stoma had shrunk; it would not accept the tube.

As a precaution when I was ordering supplies, I'd ordered the tubes in various sizes. I went to look for them now. We kept sizing down from the twelve Evan had been wearing, to the ten, to the eight, and finally were successful in inserting the six.

I knew that gradually, starting tomorrow, we would have to move up to the size twelve again.

It felt like starting all over again.

IT IS MY PERIODONTIST IN Connecticut who is going to yank both lower molars. He tells me, frankly, the teeth look fine to him, but hey, he doesn't want to argue with a guy who deals with cancer every day of the week and who's doubtless being cautious about the future. So he yanks the first tooth on 17 September. Easy come, easy go. It's only been in my mouth for six decades.

*

THE RESTAURANT THE FLAIMS TAKE us to is a Chinese joint in New Canaan, Connecticut. Angela Flaim is a beautiful woman, unmistakably Chinese. Whenever I introduce her, I always add, to her apparent amusement, 'By the way, she's Chinese.' Since she has chosen the place tonight, this provides me with an opportunity to ask if the roast dog is any good here. Angela replies at once, 'Yes, if you order the Pekinese.'

This is now four days after the extraction of the left lower front molar, but it has healed well, and I am ready to venture out in public again. However, I am not ready for the blast of noise that hits us in the face the moment we step through the front door. It is Saturday night, and the restaurant is a popular one, and we should have expected a crowd. But however excellent the roast dog may be, I cannot possibly cope with the din. I am still using my thumb to speak, you see. I am still covering the stoma with my thumb.

You already know how this works; I know I don't have to explain it again. But . . .

The stoma is about the size and shape of a pecan.

Or a large oval cabochon sapphire, take your choice.

After more than two weeks of practice – I've been at it ever since 5 September, mind you, the day after the TEP procedure – I've become pretty adept at lifting the stoma cover, and fitting my thumb snugly into that . . .

The stoma cover?

I beg your pardon?

Oh, haven't we discussed that yet?

Having no larynx is a real problem for me, of course, but it's a problem for other people as well. In fact, I find that much of the difficulty in dealing with my present condition is making the condition more comfortable for people who *don't* have holes in their throats. Why a nostril in the throat would be more offensive to anyone than a nostril in the *nose* – or for that matter the hole in our faces that is called a *mouth* – is beyond me. In fact, the Greek word for mouth *is* 'stoma'. The stoma in my throat then, can be thought of as just another mouth. Except that you don't walk around with your mouth open and people aren't obliged to look in at your tonsils. The hole in the throat looks as it might belong in a science-fiction film, a gaping hollow *gap* behind and beyond which lies the human interior, naked and frankly uninviting.

Which is why there are stoma covers, I suppose, and why people who have had laryngectomies wear them. There are large stoma covers and smaller stoma covers. There are stoma covers fashioned of cotton, or polyester, or a combination of both. There are fine-mesh stoma covers or wide-mesh stoma covers. Stoma covers come in blue or green or black or white or almost any color you can name; they even come in polka dots or paisleys. In essence, a stoma cover is a bib that hangs around your neck, fastened there with a little Velcro neckband. Stoma covers sometimes make it more difficult to breathe, but that's okay because if you breathe *too* easily you manufacture more mucus, anyway. The main problem with a stoma cover is sneezing. If a sneeze catches you unexpectedly, mucus flies out of that hole in your throat and gets all over the cover itself and your shirt and your neck and your fingers.

But aside from this minor inconvenience, it is really quite simple to slide your hand under the cover, and position your thumb over the stoma whenever you wish to talk. The captured air rushes through the prosthesis, vibrates tissues in the throat, and is shaped into words by the tongue and the mouth.

We left the Chinese restaurant and went to a Spanish restaurant in Norwalk. This was okay, too; Juan was born in Argentina. Besides, when I was able to be heard, nobody had any trouble understanding me. Even my fluent Cantonese was easily understood by Angela, who I'm sure prefers speaking Mandarin.

*

THE SECOND TOOTH COMES OUT on 24 September. Dina and I had planned a short trip to Vermont to catch the turning of the leaves, but with radiation about to begin eight days from now, we decide to stay home and relax. It is a calm and optimistic time for both of us. In fact, now that I've recovered from the minor procedure that turned out to be a major pain in the ass, I feel remarkably healthy. Who needs radiation, anyway?

GOOD TIMES AND BAD TIMES, I've seen them all, and I'm here, I'm still here . . .

Some days are terrific, others are lousy.

Some days, I can talk like an orator, others I can't find the stoma to cover with my thumb.

Some days, in fact, I sound like a fat man playing a tuba.

Some days I cough a lot.

Other days, I hardly cough at all.

Go figure.

Three days from now, I will start radiation. I've been told to expect a dry mouth (permanently) and fatigue (temporarily). The light at the end of the tunnel is that once it's over (six–seven weeks) they can then give me the valve that will cover the stoma (instead of my thumb) and allow hands-free communication in a human, Man-With-A-Cold voice.

Aluvai!

THE TRACH TUBE IS STILL a nuisance. We have progressed from the thick metal one to the less cumbersome, plastic tube. But this elbow-shaped *thing* strapped to my neck and jutting into my throat day and night must remain in place throughout the course of the radiation because the radiation may shrink the hole in my throat and that could be a problem. With radiation, everything can turn into a problem, and no one is taking any chances. But I can still take the tube out some three times a day for half an hour each time, to practice speaking by covering the stoma with my thumb. This is not as simple as it may sound. The shape of the thumb is not precisely the shape of the stoma, you see, and a great deal of fussing-and-fitting is required if I wish to avoid mere hissing. After radiation, a simple valve will do that job, opening when I breathe, closing when I speak. But that is later. In any case, even wearing the tube most of the time, I feel I am getting better and better day by day.

True, the prosthetic voice still sounds somewhat like a Chicago reporter who drinks hard and smokes a lot. But I am able to hold long conversations with Dina and our friends, and I've even tried speaking on the phone a few times (with less success, I must admit). I suppose it's the same way you get to Carnegie Hall. Practice. I'm working well, too, moving along on *The Frumious Bandersnatch* at a furious clip, some seven or eight pages every day. I am very pleased with the book, and I hope to have a good portion of it finished before 3 October, when I'll begin trotting into the city and back again every weekday.

I do not cough very much anymore.

I am not in any pain at all.

I am eating anything I want to eat.

I am almost afraid to jinx it.

ON THE WEEKEND BEFORE RADIATION is to start, we engage in a flurry of social activity, choosing small quiet restaurants, going to them with only one other couple each time.

Whenever we are to dine out, I remove the trach tube, fasten the stoma cover to my neck, and off we go!

I have become quite expert at using my thumb.

One day, like Little Jack Horner, I may order myself a Christmas pie, and stick in my thumb, and pull out a plum, and shout 'What a good boy am I!'

THE DRIVER WHO WILL TAKE us into the city has been recommended by close friends of ours. Dina spoke to him on the phone the other day and explained that we would be driving in every weekday for the next six weeks or so. She told him that we had to be in the city at 2:15, that the radiation would take about an hour or so, including waiting time, and that we'd then be driving right back to Connecticut. He said this was all fine with him, and we arranged a pickup time for today, the second day of October, at twelve noon. We still aren't certain how long it will take to get from our house, at this time of day, to the Beth Israel Medical Center on Union Square East, quite a ways downtown in New York. So we've allowed ourselves plenty of time.

The first treatment is not set to begin until the following day, but today they will be taking measurements for the actual radiation, and also fitting me for a mask that will cover my face and my chin each time the machine zaps my throat.

A mask?

This is another surprise.

Bit by bit. Morsel by morsel.

The mask will be made of a thin wire mesh. It will be placed over my face each time I come in for treatment, and then it will be clamped to a board on the table under my head. The mask will not be there to protect my face from radiation. Nothing like that. That isn't its purpose. It will be there so that my head will not move while the technicians zero in on precisely where the rays are to be directed.

It is imperative that the rays hit the right target.

These are death rays.

They are there to kill cells.

They place me on the table and mix the glop they will slap onto my face.

I am now getting quite used to the feeling of helplessness that accompanies the loss of my voice. I still carry the electro-larynx with me wherever I go because the trach tube is in my throat most of the time, and it won't allow use of the prosthesis when it's in place. Even when the tube is infrequently out, the prosthetic voice is problematic, and the electro-larynx is my insurance. I can always hold it to the discovered sweet spot on my neck, press the little button, and buzz out my wishes.

And yet, this feeling of helplessness persists.

I'm not even sure I can define it. I suppose it harks back to that day when I was sitting in the wheelchair facing the wall, and was overwhelmed by the feeling that I had been somehow excluded from the stream of humanity rushing past behind me, talking, talking, all of them talking. Concentration-camp victims must have felt that way. Singled out for treatment they had done nothing to provoke or deserve. Helpless in the hands of the people running things. Herded from here to there without reason or explanation. And eventually . . .

This is ridiculous, of course. I know that the people here are only trying to help me. They are smearing plaster on my face only so that they can make a wire mask that will later hold my head motionless while they shoot dangerous bolts of lightning into me. This is all for my own good.

They are gouging holes for my eyes and my mouth.

Don't move, please.

It will dry in a moment.

Lie still, please.

You do what they say.

They are here to help you.

FOR MY FIRST RADIATION TREATMENT on 3 October, the machine breaks down.

In my honor, I suppose.

Dina and I get there on the dot for the 2:15 appointment, but we're not out of there until 4:00, and (because of traffic) we don't get home until 7:00. The next day, same appointment time, no breakdown, but we *still* have to wait an hour and a half before I am called in to take off my shirt and put on the striped hospital gown that is the uniform here.

Using my electro-larynx, I buzz out my impatience to one of the technicians. I tell him I'm a working man, and I tell him I come in all the way from Connecticut each day, and I can't afford to spend my life in a hospital waiting room. Diego is a hip guy from the Bronx, his mother Italian, his father Hispanic. At the end of November, just about when my radiation treatment will be ending, he will be leaving for six months on a beach somewhere in the Caribbean. His partner is a young black man named Cal who has told Diego I wrote the screenplay for *The Birds*. Two days into radiation, and this is common knowledge around here; it seems the waiting-room receptionist recognized my name and spread the word. This rarely happens, believe me. But I'm glad it happened here and now.

Diego tells me, 'Man, that movie scared the shit out of me.' I tell him, 'Good, that was the idea.' (Actually, I only *thought* that was the idea. Hitchcock thought the idea was to make a movie that would play in art houses all over America.) Diego tells me some dude is supposed to come in every morning at eight-thirty, but he hasn't showed up for the past week now, so flip *him*, man!

'See you Monday at eight-thirty,' he says.

Done.

As easy as that.

IN THE CAR ON THE way home, I get an idea for a short story. I go through all the radiation, you see, and I'm given a clean bill of health, and on day #35, I'm leaving the hospital when the guy whose 8:30 A.M. appointment I usurped shoots me and kills me.

*

THE ALARM CLOCK RINGS AT 5:15, awakening me and Dina, who insists on coming in to the city with me each morning. It is the seventh day of October. In a bit more than a week, I will be seventy-six years old. In all my life, the only time I've ever been awake this early was while I was serving in the Navy. It occurs to me that when my father was a mailman, he used to get up at 5:00 and go to sleep at 9:00. I became a writer so I could meet girls and sleep late. I finally met *the* Girl, but now I can't sleep late anymore. (What goes around comes around, right, Gary?)

The driver recommended by our friends is a cranky old man of the sort I hope never to become. Actually, he is probably some ten years younger than I am (and he still has his larynx!) but he seems like a hundred and four, a crotchety little fuss-budget who snarls at every other driver on the road and mutters things to himself like, 'I *hate* to drive behind SUVs,' even though our car – the one he is driving – is a Mercedes ML 320. We have arranged to be picked up between 6:15 and 6:30, depending on the weather. We figure it will take a minimum of an hour and a half to get into the city at this early hour of the morning, max two hours if the traffic is heavy.

That first day of the new schedule, we are on Union Square East at a quarter to eight. Our driver complains about having to wait downstairs at the curb, fearful he will get a ticket, but we assure him that wheelchair patients are constantly moving in and out of the center, and he reluctantly agrees to sit there. Ten minutes later, he has parked the car in the center's under-ground garage – at five bucks every fifteen minutes – and has joined us in the waiting room.

This is the routine.

You sit in the waiting room until a cheerful, friendly, ebullient nurse named Jill opens the door to the inner office, calls your name, and says, 'You can change now, Evan.'

Somehow, you do not mind her calling you 'Evan'.

Inside the door, and just to the left of it, there is a smaller waiting area with a bench against the wall. Men and women in striped gowns are sitting on that bench. Farther down the hall are rows of lockers and two small changing rooms. Because I will have only my head and neck radiated, I do not have to take off my trousers. I pluck one of the dressing gowns from its shelf (they are stacked according to size: small, medium, large), enter one of the dressing rooms, take off my sweater and shirt (this is still only October, and a mild one at that) put on the gown (the large one is too big; I exchange it for a medium), tie it up the back (they always tie up the back, so that if you are naked in Medland, your ass is showing to the world at large) and then hang up my street clothes in one of the lockers, and go to join the other cancer patients sitting on the bench.

When Diego or Cal come out for you, you follow them back to the radiation room.

You lie on a metal table that is covered with a sheet. You are fully dressed. Trousers, socks, shoes, and the striped hospital gown tied in the back. They take your wire-mesh mask from a cubbyhole on a shelf bearing similar masks and they carry it to where you are lying flat on your back, and then they clamp the mask to the board under your head and insert a flat white tongue depressor into your mouth. You bite down on this stick, holding it upright. You can look cross-eyed through the eye slits in the mask and see illuminated markings appearing on the stick, projected there by the machine. You do not really know what is going on, but you assume they are somehow using this stick to make their calibrations. They will position the machine using the marks on the stick as a guide.

You feel like the Man in the Iron Mask.

You want to make a joke about your father being the best swordsman in France.

You wonder if they are too young to have seen the movie.

You are sure your beard will grow inside the mask, eventually suffocating you.

You have been told your beard will no longer grow on the radiated areas of your neck.

The machine is a huge monster. Diego and Cal lean over you, moving the head of the looming machine this way and that.

'Are you on?'

'I'm on.'

They are reading figures or marks only they can see. Your head is nailed to that board, you cannot turn it to see what they're actually consulting, what figures or marks they're reading. All of this is computerized, you understand, all of these measurements are made the first time you walked into this room, all of them were fed into the computer, and now only the technicians know what they're doing. Once again, your future health, your very life, is in the hands of strangers.

When they are satisfied they have positioned the machine exactly where it should be . . .

'Forgive me, I am very fussy.'

. . . they leave the room. From behind their protective shield, they twist dials (you suppose) and throw switches (you suppose) and there is a brief pause, and then a hum, and the machine begins working, and the invisible rays begin invading your body.

THERE IS A FLOWERING TREE painted on the ceiling above the machine. For the next thirty-five days, for about two minutes on each of those days, you will peer up at that tree through the slitted holes in your restraining mask. You are still wearing the trach tube. There is a tongue depressor in your mouth. You are fearful you will have a coughing fit and be unable to move your head. So you use the tree as a calming influence, searching among the petals of its flowers for the hidden faces among them.

There is a virtual Planet of the Apes buried in the white blossoms of the tree. As the machine hums and the rays fly, you search for the faces formed by the petals. You find eyes and noses and mouths. You find monkeys and gorillas and chimps. You even find, of all things, a long-eared white rabbit lurking there in the branches of this wondrous tree.

And you count.

The minute the machine starts humming, you start counting.

Ah-*one*, ah-*two*, ah-*three*, ah-*four* . . .

Each of these ah-*booms* signifies a second.

Ah-*twenty*, ah-*one*, ah-*two*, ah-*three* . . .

Ah-*thirty*, ah-*one*, ah . . .

And the machine quits, more or less after thirty seconds. You pride yourself on calculating the seconds correctly. Sometimes, the machine will cut off when you've counted only to twenty-eight or nine. Sometimes, it will cut off at thirty-five. The machine is never wrong, the machine is computerized. It is only your counting that is more or less accurate. At thirty seconds, only one side of your neck is done. The head of the machine moves over to the other side. The technicians come in again, make their calculations. Leave the room. Silence. And the machine starts humming again.

Ah-*one*, ah-*two* . . .

There, another face among the blossoms!

A smiling monkey.

They zap you for thirty seconds on one side of your neck, thirty seconds on the other, and a full-frontal minute on the spot where your Adam's apple used to be.

What with strapping your head down, and positioning the machine and all, you're on the table for perhaps a total of fifteen minutes each time.

But you've been here at the center since eight this morning, and you rarely get out of here before nine-thirty.

There's a Starbucks downstairs.

You buy Dina and yourself a cappuccino and head uptown.

*

191

WE SHOOT STRAIGHT UP PARK Avenue and arrive outside Slavit's office on Seventy-fourth Street in ten minutes flat. It is still only nine-forty. I figure we'll be out of here in five minutes and on the parkway ten minutes after that. Home and at my desk by twelve noon, easy. *Bandersnatch*, here I come!

'Alex,' I say, 'we just have to pick up a prescription. If you'll wait right here . . .'

Alex's bald head whips around. His blue eyes flash.

With a vehemence he usually reserves for drivers of SUVs, he snaps, 'No, I *won't* wait right here!'

My mouth falls open.

'Maybe *you* want a ticket,' he says, 'but *I* don't. I'll just drive around the block till I see you.'

There is absolutely no danger of his getting a ticket here. There are doctors' offices all up and down the avenue, and limos are parked alongside the curb everywhere.

'Fine, Alex,' I say, and get out of the car, and wait for Dina to join me on the sidewalk, and then slam the door shut behind us.

I hope Alex realizes he's just been fired.

WHEN WE TELL OUR GOOD friends Liz Fuller and her husband Reuel Dorman what happened with our driver, they both say at once, 'Fire him.' I tell them he's already been fired. Reuel then suggests that his son John might be able to drive us in every morning.

John Dorman is a young man in his late twenties, a professional shortstop with the Bridgeport Bluefish. In the off-season, and this is now officially the off-season, he serves as a substitute teacher at a local elementary school where his hours are flexible. He foresees no problem with having to get up at the crack of dawn, and on Monday morning, the fourteenth day of October and the eighth day of my radiation therapy, he rolls into our driveway at 6:15 A.M., parks his car, and hops behind the wheel of the Mercedes. We are on our way five minutes later.

The *New York Times* has just been dropped into our mailbox. In the back seat of the Mercedes truck, Dina reads the paper. In the front seat, I curl up with a pillow and sleep until we turn off the East River Drive at the 23rd Street exit.

John doesn't find any problem in waiting at the curb with the other cars parked there.

I am on the table at 9:07.

THAT TUESDAY (THE DAY HARRISON makes his 'status' rounds, and coincidentally the fifteenth of October – birth date of great men, he thought but did not say) I am told that instead of thirty-*five* treatments, I will be receiving only thirty-*three*. This is good news. Every patient in this place counts the days. Today is treatment number nine for me, which means only twenty-four to go, which means (at five days a week) I'll be finished on 18 November. In time to celebrate a *real* Thanksgiving. In the meantime, today is my birthday (as if you didn't guess) and Dina and I have good cause to celebrate right now.

There have been no side effects so far, and I'm determined not to have any.

I am seventy-six years old and in good health.

I feel great and I look terrific.

Dina always looks terrific, and she's a rock.

And I have only twenty-four days to go before the end of radiation.

ON THE BENCH INSIDE SUITE 4G at Beth Israel, we sit together and await our turns on the machines.

Most of the men on this bench have prostate cancer.

In the year 2002, there are more than a million cancer victims in the United States. Half of those victims died, more than 1500 people a day.

1500 people a day.

Most of the female victims had breast cancer.

Some 200,000 of them.

Most of the men had prostate cancer.

189,000 of them.

The majority of men and women here for radiation treatment have either breast or prostate cancer.

The men look like hapless actors in some low-budget porn flick, wearing shoes and socks and the striped gown tied up the back, no trousers, no shirts.

One of them tells me he has to inject his penis with a needle every time he wants an erection.

'Least I can get one,' he says, and grins.

There are two girls wearing head scarves on that bench.

One is a beautiful black girl who tells me she manages a Victoria's Secret shop uptown. She has had chemotherapy already, and is now trying radiation. She knows that an estimated 40,000 women will die of breast cancer this year.

The other Girl in a Scarf must have been a blonde when she still had hair. Her complexion is fair, her eyes blue. She wears no makeup, not even lipstick. The blue scarf matches her eyes. She tells me she got furious this morning when a man outside her building started fighting her for a taxi.

Pressing my electro-larynx to my neck, I ask *So what did you do?*

'I played the Cancer Card,' she says, and grins conspiratorially.

The Cancer Card.

A black woman with cancer of the sinuses introduces herself as Alicia. She tells me she's a registered nurse. She tells me her daughter is a doctor.

'Are you the one who wrote *The Birds*?' she asks.

'I'm the one.'

'And you look like such a nice man,' she says teasingly. 'Listen, I think we both get here around the same time, so here's what we should do.'

She then goes on to outline a plan whereby whichever one of us gets here first, we should change and go right in to the machine, instead of paying attention to who's supposed to go in at what time.

I tell her that sounds like a good idea.

'Good,' she says, and nods. 'It's what we'll do.'

There is one man here who has cancer of the eyes. A tall Indian man who brings his small boy to the waiting room with him one day.

Only one other man has had his larynx removed. There will be an estimated 9000 cases of cancer of the larynx reported this year. A third of those will die. Speech is enormously difficult for him. He fumbles for a pad and pencil and scribbles what he wants to say.

I smoked two packs a day, he writes.

Five years ago, when Dr. Ghossein was fussily directing his healing rays at the tattoo mark on my Adam's apple, everybody else had cancer but I didn't.

Now I no longer have an Adam's apple.

I am a cancer patient.

I am one of them.

A non-joiner, I have joined the club.

WHEN I BUY DINA HER cappuccino that morning, I tell her I don't think it's necessary for her to come in with me every day from now on.

She protests.

But I can tell she's relieved.

*

THE ROUTINE IS UNVARYING.

John and I have the route into the city down pat. We know exactly where to expect bottlenecks, exactly where the traffic will be moving freely. He now picks me up at 6:30 each morning, we exchange greetings and pleasantries, and then I collapse onto my pillow and fall asleep until we hit the 23rd Street exit off the Drive. Rarely do we arrive at the hospital later than 8:45. I go upstairs, walk right into the inner waiting room without stopping at the reception desk, check to see if Alicia's already there, and then either go straight into the machine, or sit down to wait for her to be finished with her treatment.

After the zapping, Jill weighs me and spritzes my throat with saline. I don't know why she does this. It is all part of the mysterious routine. A not-so-mysterious part of the routine is buying myself a cappuccino at the Starbucks on the corner before climbing into the car where John is waiting for me. One day, an NYPD cop gives him a parking ticket. I tell him he should have played the cancer card.

I am wide awake on the way home to Connecticut. I am still working on *The Frumious Bandersnatch*, and my working day begins the moment I step into that Mercedes truck. Sipping my cappuccino, I scribble brief cryptic notes on paper napkins from Starbucks.

'She saw my face!' Kellie said.

Or:

Wasteland, why?
Deserted.
Clear sight lines.
Show off the dead dog.

Or:

Heart-heart talk.
End with: 'It was starting to
get dark.'

Bit by bit.
And soon . . .
Before I knew it . . .

Friday, November 8, 2002

Hello, dear people.

Believe it or not, there are only six more treatments to go! Six. Count 'em. Six.

Five next week, and then one on Monday, November 18th, and that is it, kiddies. I can sleep late again, the way a writer should.

It has been quite an experience. My hidden desire was to get out of there one morning before nine. Impossible. There is always something. Either the guy who's supposed to 'warm up' the machine doesn't show up on time, or the machine's 'little gas cylinder' wasn't replaced last night and we have to wait for someone to bring one down . . . always something. I have never gotten out of there by nine o'clock, even though I'm always there by eight-fifteen. Never. So much for impossible dreams.

There have been very few side effects. They told me I would turn lobster red by treatment #15, but Friday was treatment #27, and nothing like that has happened. Mild burning is all, rather like what you get after an hour on the beach. Eased by the application of something called Aquaphor, which in itself sounds like a disease.

One day I had difficulty swallowing, but they gave me a pill for that, and I've been eating very well ever since – aren't you thrilled by all these details? The thing is it's been

a piece of cake, as they say, or a walk in the park as they
further say, except for getting up at five-thirty and driving
into the city, and delaying my work day till roughly eleven
each morning.

I've had the voice prosthesis in place since September
sometime, but I still have to cover the hole in my throat
with my thumb in order to force air through the device, and
produce speech. This will change once I'm through with the
radiation. They could not fit me with an open-and-close
valve because tissue shrinks during radiation and they have
to take exact measurements. But once the valve is in place,
it will stay open when I breathe, and close when I speak,
and it will also have a filter on it which will keep germs and
carbon monoxide and such from going directly into my
lungs, as is their wont. Hands-free speech and a filter
besides! What more could anyone ask for?

And remember. Only six more days!

So thanks for hanging around and listening to all this. I
truly appreciate your concern. I'll probably let you know
what happens after I've caught up on my sleep.
Meanwhile, all best,
Evan

I FEEL LIKE J.K. ROWLING.

On my Starbucks napkins, I scribble this:

Carella feels like a jackass.
Shouldn't be here!
What the hell am I doing here?
Pissing with the big dogs now!

Or this:

Rookie flashback.

Or this:

John: Radio Shack pre-paid cell phone.
$55 a month.

Morsel by morsel.

Monday, November 11, 2002

Now pay attention, kiddies!

Five more to go. Only five!

And this morning, I got off the second machine at nine o'clock sharp.

But . . .

Does this mean I got out of Beth Israel at nine o'clock sharp? Nay, kiddies.

Because then I had to get weighed and sprayed (they spritz my throat after each treatment) and then I had to change into my street clothes from my gown (no, not the long black one with the pearls, but a striped hospital gown that always seems to have one of the ties missing) and then I had to call down for the car before the NYPD (unmindful that the car is ED McBAIN's!) ticketed the driver again, and then I had to buy a cup of coffee at Starbucks, and so I was on my way out of the city by 9:10 A.M.

Close, but no cigar.

I'm still trying.

I've got five more days to do it!

I CONFIDED THIS SECRET DESIRE to Diego and Cal.

Which was why, on the last day of radiation, Monday, 18 November, I would have been downstairs and in the truck by nine on the dot, if Alicia and the Girl in the Scarf hadn't brought in copies of *The Moment She Was Gone* for me to sign.

I hugged them both close, but not because they were among

the scant dozen people who'd bought my latest Evan Hunter effort. We hugged because over the past thirty-three days, in this cloistered setting that was Suite 4G of the Radiation Oncology Clinic at Beth Israel Hospital, we had become a true band of brothers and sisters, united by our illness, and now about to go our separate ways, cancer-free (we hoped) into what might sometimes be an uncertain future.

Good luck, we told each other.

Stay well, we told each other.

There were still tears in my eyes when I told the counter girl at Starbucks that I wanted a grande cappuccino, please, very dry, please, and could she please drop this Equal into the bottom of the cup?

6

SO TO SPEAK

IN THE WAITING ROOM OF MEETH's voice clinic, on one of my recent visits there, I ran into a guy who was still using the electro-larynx; the configuration of his stoma made it impossible for him to use any of the other speaking devices. He started telling me his history. When he discovered he had cancer of the larynx, his choice was clear. Remove the larynx or die. Lose your voice or lose your life. Keep your larynx and end up in a coffin.

'The vox or the box,' he said.

He had not chosen the box. And he sounded good on the electro-larynx, clearly understandable, but maybe that was only because I'd been there before.

Nobody promised us a rose garden, you see, nobody took us aside and said, 'The reason we're taking out your larynx is so you'll be able to speak better.'

What they said was, 'We're taking out your larynx so the cancer won't kill you.'

The vox or the box?

Choose.

We chose life, of course.

We chose to live.

BUT I AM DISCOVERING THAT there are certain realities to this – what shall I call it?

Condition?

There are certain realities to this condition of mine.

No, I don't think I like that.

There are certain realities to this *life* I must now lead.

These realities may be termed 'minor inconveniences', I suppose. And none of them should stop me from enjoying a normal life, correct? I will get used to them, correct?

For example, I can no longer lift heavy things.

So? Big deal.

What it is, when they remove your larynx, you lose ten to twenty percent of your lifting power, did you know that? You ever see these massive weight-lifters straining to hoist a barbell? You notice those bulging cords in their necks? They're 'locking up the larynx', as we call it in the trade, giving themselves that extra little lifting power they need. But if you don't have a larynx, you can't very well lock it, now can you? Well, so what? I never lifted heavy things, anyway. And what if I now have to stand by feeling boorish while Dina carries the heavy groceries in from the car? My mother taught me otherwise – but laryngectomy has gone her one better. Sorry, Mom, but if someone asks me to move a piano, I'll just have to decline.

My peripheral vision is shot, too.

There are now scars in my throat from when they were cutting all that tissue and muscle, and I can't turn my head as easily as I used to. To see to my left or right, I now have to turn my shoulders rather than just my head. To look down, I have to get past that scar tissue first. So I find myself bumping into things, or tripping over things, or knocking over stemmed glasses because my neck mobility is limited and whereas I'm moving as fast as I used to, my head can't catch up with my hands or my feet.

I sometimes throw up.

If I bend over too swiftly, food I've just swallowed (or *thought* I'd just swallowed) will tend to rise into my throat. That's because when they took my larynx, they also removed the upper esophageal sphincter. This is the muscle at the top of the esophagus, the tube leading down to the stomach. Since this is no longer there, food goes directly down the esophagus where it is assisted into the stomach by the *lower* esophageal sphincter, at the opposite end of the tube. Without that upper muscle there to keep the food down, it remains in the esophagus, and can easily come up again. But Dr. Sarah Stackpole at MEETH has prescribed Prevacid for this reflux, as it's called, and it helps. Sometimes. Well, most of the time.

Another inconvenience is the fluoride. Every night, before I go to sleep, I have to insert a flouride gel into these little plastic trays Dr. Verona made for me. The trays fit over my upper and lower teeth, and I must keep them in place for five minutes. Ah-*one*, ah-*two*, ah-*three*, and so on. The fluoride treatment has nothing to do with the removal of my larynx. It is just another pain in the ass that has only to do with the fact that I endured thirty-three days of radiation, and – since this was radiation of the head and neck, the teeth and gums may have been affected. So if I ever develop any kind of infection, it simply won't heal, and that would be bad news indeed. The fluoride will prevent infection.

This is what I have to do before I go to sleep each night.

I take my Prevacid (for the reflux) and my Mevacor (to keep my cholesterol low).

Then I brush my teeth.

(Well, everyone does. Big deal.)

Then I put in the fluoride trays.

While I'm counting the minutes, Dina explores my throat with her flashlight, and picks out the mucus, dried and soft.

When the five minutes are up, I remove the trays and squirt saline into the stoma. This is a 0.9 per cent sodium chloride solution that comes in these little pink sterile vials. I twist off the top, squirt the stuff into my throat, and cough up any remaining mucus. Dina then uses a little brush that resembles a miniature bottle-washing brush to apply nystatin to the prosthesis. This is to prevent yeast forming on it. One last time, she twirls the end of this little brush into the hole in the prosthesis, cleaning out any remaining debris there. This all takes some twenty minutes or so.

I am ready to go to bed.

But hold.

Some ten minutes later, mucus has already formed in my throat, and I take a final cough before settling down for the night.

When I wake up each morning, I never know if the prosthesis is going to work. I place my thumb over the hole in my throat, and try a tentative 'Hello' and either I get the actual word itself, 'Hello, hello!' or more precisely, ''Ello, 'ello!'.

It's difficult to aspirate an 'H', you see. I can't even say my own *name*! It comes out 'Evan 'Unter'. You can't imagine how many times I have to repeat my last name. 'Hunter! *Hunter!*' (Don't get angry, Evan, you can't shout remember?) And finally spelling it, 'H-U-N-T-E-R'. Which comes out '*Aysh*-ooo-N-T-E-R'. (I'm thinking of changing it legally to McBain, which I can easily pronounce. Won't be the first time I've gone through *that* process, either.)

But every morning, I get either ''Ello, 'ello!' and I grin gratefully, or else I just get air rushing against the prosthesis in a futile hiss. I never know which it will be. If I cannot speak because the prosthesis is clogged with dried mucus, or has somehow twisted out of position, how will I be able to phone the police or the fire department? I call for Dina instead. That is to say, I do not *call* for her because one cannot call if one has no voice, hmm, my dear Watson?

What I do is ring the Fight Bell. When we got married, our good friends Dick and Charlotte Condon gave us a glass bell which we were told either one of us could pick up and shake whenever we wanted to end an argument. Dina and I have rarely had to use the Fight Bell. But now I grab for it whenever I can't talk, and shake it. Wherever she may be – downstairs in the kitchen, out in the garden, at her desk, wherever – she calls at once, 'Right away, honey!' and in a few moments she's peering into my throat with a flashlight, and then poking around in there with tweezers or a brush, plucking out mucus, freeing the prosthesis, freeing the words.

'Thank you, darling,' I say.

I say this even though quite often the poking and probing is painful. In fact, almost everything about having no larynx is painful at worst, or uncomfortable at best. There is never truly a moment in my life when I am not aware of my neck or my throat. The pain is always there. It is not what I would call terrible pain. But there is almost always mild pain.

(*Mild* pain? What is *mild* pain? Is it like being a little bit pregnant?)

Mild pain is pain that's a nuisance.

A minor inconvenience, so to speak.

Sometimes it's a sharp sudden pain in the area of the prosthesis. I guess this is due to the fact that there's a foreign object in my throat. If the prosthesis is removed, the TEP (I refuse to type 'tracheoesophageal puncture' ever again, as long as I live!) will close. The body naturally seeks to close wounds, remember? And the TEP is a wound. So I guess the body knows that a vinyl thing is stuck in my esophagus there, and every now and then it gives me a little reminding twinge of protest. And because the anatomy is all somehow connected up there, I sometimes get pain in my ears or my shoulders, go ask. I'm not a doctor. I just know that the pain is there, mild but constant.

In addition to the pain, there is always a tight, constricted feeling about the neck. This is caused by whatever I've got glued over the stoma at any particular time. What I wear around the house is a little flapping piece of foam sponge that comes in white or buff and that has a thin strip of adhesive along its top. I stick this onto my neck, and either press my thumb tight over it and against the stoma when I want to talk, or else I reach under it with my thumb. Either way, the adhesive strip sort of gathers the skin, and pinches it some-what, so that I'm always aware of it. My neck is no longer that carefree swanlike thing sitting there between my head and my shoulders; it's now something that constantly *reminds* me it's there.

There is almost always something glued over the stoma.

Either this little hanging sponge – which is the least intrusive – or else the larger piece of adhesive that holds the plastic ring into which I insert either the valve I must press to talk, or the so-called hands-free valve, which requires applying silicone glue to both the adhesive patch and the skin.

I can live with the pain.

As I said, it's not excruciating.

I can also live with having adhesives stuck to my throat all the time.

I can't drink alcoholic beverages anymore. Dr. Harrison has told me that drinking may cause either the recurrence of old cancer cells or the growth of new ones. I didn't believe him at first. But whenever I have a glass of wine and Dina looks into my throat the next morning, there is dried blood lining the passage to my lungs. It's one thing to *guess* at what's happening in there. It's another thing to take an actual look inside and *see* the results. But I never was a heavy drinker, anyway, so giving up alcohol is no tremendous loss. You get used to it.

Whenever I eat chocolate, it clogs the prosthesis and causes coughing.

Whenever I drink a cappuccino, it leaks through the prosthesis and causes coughing.

If I step from a colder room into a heated room, I start coughing.

If I step from a heated space into an air-conditioned one, I start coughing.

The car's heater starts me coughing. So does the car's air-conditioner.

Even when I just open the refrigerator door, I begin coughing.

And remember the Swimmer's Ear? The itching that first caused me to visit Dr. Cyclops back in 1992?

Well, my ears still itch.

(In fact, I think they itch even more after the radiation.)

But none of this is too difficult to live with.

What's really hard is . . .

The silence.

I have lost my voice, you see.

That is the very worst part.

All at once, my true voice is gone.

That very special and unique part of me that was the way I sounded is utterly and completely gone.

With a prosthesis, I find that I don't chatter as much as I used to.

I sometimes forget what I wanted to say because by the time I cover the stoma to talk, the thought is gone.

I think a lot.

I'm alone a lot in my silence.

I've lost my patience for petty bullshit. I find small talk boring and enormously difficult; my tolerance gives out even before my voice does. Given this newfound talent for summary dismissal, I try not to bore listeners with tales of my own current medical status, and resist the temptation to ask, 'Wanna look in at my prosthesis?'

(But tell me, Mrs. Lincoln . . . aside from all that, how did you enjoy the play?)

Well, there are blessings.

I don't have to wear a tie anymore. Even at formal gatherings, I can play the Cancer Card and show them the hole in my throat. Nobody wants me to suffocate because a tie is covering that hole.

I can no longer smell anything. The sense of smell went

south with my larynx. So save your rotten fish or other noxious odors. They faze me not in the slightest.

I can kiss my wife for hours without once having to draw a breath. That's because I breathe through my throat.

And, oh yes, I no longer snore.

I can't think of any other blessings.

But I'm sure I will.

As time goes by, I'm sure I will.

I MAKE SURE THAT THE house is free of dust.

I start a fire in the fireplace long before Evan enters the room. Even so, holding hands while watching the fire sometimes has to be interrupted because smoke is reaching my husband's throat.

I wear perfume only occasionally, and when I do put it on, I clear the air in the room immediately afterward.

We do not use liquids in spray bottles to clean the house.

I've replaced all sharp-smelling chemicals with diluted vinegar and lemon-scented water.

All our washing is done with non-perfumed washing powder, very little of it, and we repeat the rinse two or three times, depending on how close the fabric will come to my husband's stoma.

Because of the radiation, Evan's skin is very sensitive, so we have bid goodbye to starched sheets. We do our ironing with lavender water instead. This way, the bedding is soft and it smells of Provence.

We never go to bed without a humidifier. There is a humidifier right next to my husband's desk, too.

I keep gentle soap and shampoo for him in the shower, but his skin still gets irritated. So, we tried fresh egg instead, and it helped. Our friends, Jane Powell and Dick Moore, recommended that we try vitamin E. It was enormously helpful. We apply it now regularly, as a precaution.

Our lifestyle has changed.

IN MY LIFE, REMAINING MUTE is not an option.

My wife calls me a little 'chatterbox', an American word she picked up somewhere along the way. A little chatterbox. Just try to keep a chatterbox from speaking. Besides, I *must* speak. I am a writer. I must read to people from my books. I must do a Q&A and be bright and witty and charming. I must *talk* to people while I'm signing books. I must *speak*!

Well, there are now two types of speech I can enjoy.

The constant in the artificial speech mechanism is the tiny vinyl prosthesis in my esophagus. This is no euphemism. It truly is tiny, no larger than a quarter of an inch in diameter. Years ago, this had to be changed daily. Removed from the throat, cleaned, replaced. A necessary routine, like brushing your teeth. (In Medland, all daily medical routines are likened to 'brushing your teeth'. The dentists of America must be thrilled.) Nowadays, the prosthesis is what they call 'indwelling', embedded there in the esophagus for anything like four to six months before it has to be replaced by a clinician.

As you know, the way the prosthesis works is you force air through it by covering the stoma with your thumb. As you further know, you can wear a stoma cover over this charming but unsightly hole, offering the world polka dots and paisley instead of an unsolicited glimpse of *Alien 3* residing inside your throat. The stoma cover may be pretty to view, but it's difficult to manipulate when you have to sneeze or cough. Besides, it does little to alleviate the basic problem caused by a total laryngectomy.

The problem – as it's been explained to me only 2034 times – is that a total laryngectomy not only eliminates a person's ability to speak, it also takes away the function of his nose. The nose is now a gorgeous but essentially useless ornament on the face. It no longer inhales air. Which means that the air you breathe is no longer heated or humidified. Neither is it filtered. And – probably most important – because you are breathing air directly into your lungs, without the middlemen of nose or mouth – there is less *resistance* to breathing. The body knows this. How does it know?

I don't know how it knows.

But it knows.

And it compensates for this loss by performing what is known as 'pulmonary rehabilitation'. The symptoms of this instinctive rehab are:

Excessive mucus production
Coughing
Forced expectoration.

So the various companies involved in pulmonary rehabilitation have come up with some devices designed to encourage the heating and moisturizing of inhaled air, and – oh yes – to make speaking easier.

Once again: when the hole in my throat is open, I breathe air into my lungs.

When the hole is closed, expelled air is forced instead through the prosthesis and into my mouth, where it is shaped into speech – just the way people with larynxes magically spin air into words. To partially filter the air I breathe, I can wear that hanging foam patch I've already described, or I can use one of two currently available devices to cover and close the stoma.

Both of these devices are valves that fasten to the throat with an adhesive patch that has a plastic housing built into it. The patch has the appearance and consistency of a large Band-Aid. Each of the valves is designed to fit snugly into the housing on the patch. It takes no more than a minute to swab the area around the hole first with alcohol and then with a topical preparation that leaves the area somewhat tacky. It takes just another minute to peel off the back of the patch and smooth it onto the skin. It is now ready to receive the valve.

The first of the valves is merely a plastic disc about the size of a quarter, an inch or so in diameter, an eighth of an inch wide. Called an HME – for Heat and Moisture Exchanger – it is nothing more than a filtering baffle with tiny vents along its sides. The normal 'open' position of this little valve allows air to pass in through the small venting slits, get filtered through the waffle-like sponge, and pass from there down into my lungs, cleaner and moister and warmer.

The lid is in the 'closed' position when I press down on it. This prevents new air from entering through the vents, and directs trapped air through the prosthesis instead.

Do you see how it works?

I just press the little plastic button stuck to my throat, and I can talk.

I consider this nothing short of miraculous, truly.

When it works, I feel wonderful.

I feel normal.

But there are times when using this becomes awkward or simply embarrassing.

I'm at the supermarket checkout.

I'm putting my credit card back into my wallet, an operation that requires both hands.

The checkout girl says, 'Thank you, sir. Have a nice day.'

I can't answer her for several moments because I can't bring either hand to my throat to press that button.

She thinks I'm merely being rude.

Or, I'm on the telephone.

My left hand grips the receiver, my right hand presses the button every time I want to talk. But what happens when I have to take notes on the conversation? Where's that third hand when you really need it? And how often can you explain to the stranger who's just repeated a telephone number four times, 'Gee, sorry, I can't speak and write at the same time.'

The second type of valve is a hands-free device that looks like a tiny plastic mushroom cap. It, too, fits snugly into the plastic housing fastened to the throat. Bulkier than the other valve, rounded where the other one is flat, it contains a curved elastic membrane that unrolls when air is exhaled, closing the side openings of the valve and re-directing the airflow through the voice prosthesis to produce speech. Moreover, it can be fastened to another sort of heat and moisture exchanger, a narrow baffle that condenses exhaled air and evaporates it into the inhaled air. In effect, this valve is a substitute nose, mouth and throat combined with substitute vocal cords!

In fact, when the hands-free valve works, it seems like the ultimate solution. Who needs a larynx, anyway? Just do the alcohol swab, slap on the preparation that makes the skin stickier, fasten the adhesive patch . . .

Wait a minute, wait a minute.

Because the hands-free valve requires forceful air pressure to redirect the air, the adhesive patch has to be fastened quite securely to the throat. Otherwise the seal will break, and you'll get hissing air instead of intelligible speech. This means that in addition to the usual cleaning and preparatory routine, you have to brush a silicone glue onto both the skin and the adhesive patch. It's like using Superglue on a piece of broken crockery. You slap it onto both surfaces. Here, however, one of those surfaces happens to be human flesh. (Mine, by the way!) Moreover, it is flesh that was recently radiated for thirty-three days and is therefore, shall we say, still extremely sensitive? Besides, whenever the patch is peeled off the throat, you have to use a solvent – which works like nail-polish remover, and probably contains the same ingredients – to clean the skin of glue and whatever other *shmutz* has accumulated under the patch while you were wearing it. The solvent further irritates the skin, and makes the entire hands-free experience less desirable than it seemed when you first pitched it to the network.

Right now, I cannot imagine wearing either of these valves while reading the first chapter of a new novel to a bookstore crowd. In fact, I can barely imagine wearing either of them to a *restaurant*!

What if a sneeze ambushes me?

With a cough, the mucus is merely propelled to the rim of the stoma . . .

This is disgusting, I know.

But think about how much *more* disgusting it would be in a restaurant or at a friend's dinner table. This is what I think about all the time. This is what stops me from going out. Suppose I cough up mucus while I'm dining out with relatives or friends? I have only two hands. I no longer wear a tie, but even with an open-throat shirt, a cough requires some fast maneuvering.

I normally carry my handkerchief in the right-hand back pocket of my trousers. Okay – here comes the cough. Left hand goes to the collar of the shirt to move it aside. Right hand goes for the handkerchief in that back pocket. Now comes the prestidigitation! Whatever's covering the stoma must be dealt with before the handkerchief can effectively do its thing.

If it's the foam flap, this has to be lifted with the forefinger of the right hand so that the handkerchief can cover the stoma before the offending mucus is expelled. If it's the simple filtering valve, this has to be yanked from its housing with the left hand, *after* the hand has moved the collar aside, so that the right hand can quickly reach up with the handkerchief. And if it's the hands-free valve, the operation becomes particularly complicated because that little mushroom cap is difficult to remove.

Better to send out for Chinese, no?

Yes!

SNEEZING IS THE MOST DIFFICULT to control.

You cannot prepare for a sneeze. It just comes. Do you know that your heart stops when you sneeze? Little known fact, but true. It's like being dead for a second. It's also like being mortified for a second if you happen to sneeze mucus onto someone's shirt front or into someone's soup. So how can I go to a restaurant or a dinner party?

I can't.

How can I possibly control a sneeze?

I can't.

The first thing you have to remember about coughing or sneezing is that you don't cover your nose or your mouth. This is not where the mucus is coming from. It is coming from that hole in your throat. Where once there was just a single railroad controlled by the switch that was your larynx, there are now two separate railroads, one leading from your mouth to your stomach, the other from your stoma to your lungs. The Mouth-Stomach Railway produces saliva. The Stoma-Lungs Railroad produces mucus. You can spit out saliva, but you can only cough up mucus.

Contrary to expectations, my saliva glands haven't been affected by the radiation. I am producing plenty of saliva and my mouth isn't ever dry. In fact, sometimes there is too damn *much* saliva. Which is another obstacle to dining out. Either you cough or you sneeze or you gurgle and none of these options is acceptable in polite society. A running nose is another problem. You cannot blow your nose except by doing what one of the laryngectomee self-help manuals describes thus: 'Pinch your nostrils with a handkerchief. Close your mouth. Move your lower jaw in a vigorous chewing motion while simultaneously raising your tongue to the roof of your mouth in a piston-like motion. This will drive the air through your nose and the pinched nostrils will further compress the escaping air so as to clear the nose of any matter. Try it!' Not on your life, bro! Can you imagine performing such nasal-digital calisthenics in your local restaurant!

All in all, it's best to stay home, right?

Right.

WE HAVE A LOT TO be grateful for on this Thanksgiving Day. My Son, Mark, and his new bride Sophie have flown over from Paris to be with us, and we are joined by Duša (Doo-shuh) and Voja (Voy-uh) Psonček (Sahn-chek), Yugoslavian friends of Dina's from way back, and now close friends of mine as well. They bring with them their newborn baby boy, Antonio, and their beautiful, lively, and imaginative daughters, Ana and Nina, aged ten and twelve.

The girls want to know all about my laryngectomy, but once I've explained it to them, they shrug it aside, and together we immediately invent a new persona for me, some sort of medieval king who has a Thing in his Throat that allows him to talk. Since the voice is husky and deep, he is – of course – a blustering villain, threatening to banish these little princesses to the dungeons whenever they erupt into spontaneous giggles. They are both marvelous actresses, and we stay in character all afternoon. Antonio becomes Antonio Bandolini, the crown prince of the kingdom. He pretends to have a cell phone into which he gurgles commands. I have not had such fun in a long time.

My daughter-in-law is a Parisienne and naturally speaks French. My son is a journalist who speaks fluent French with an outrageous, American French-fries accent. Both Voja and Duša have lived in many European countries, and both speak French as well. My dearest Dina lived in Paris for close to fifteen years, and is also fluent. There is much to talk about and the conversation is spirited and lively. My own French is limited to *Ou sont les toilettes?* but I have to admit that when I'm not being the villainous monarch, with my new voice I sound very much like a *boulevardier*. All I need is a straw boater, white spats, and a cane.

It's an easy, relaxed day.

Maybe I'm ready to venture into New York again, eh, *cherie*?

Well . . . maybe.

THE IMAGINARY CITY IN MY 87th Precinct novels is an exaggerated New York, appropriately but affectionately called the Big Bad City. Noise, crowds, traffic, jostling, pushing, shoving, the usual. Well, the real New York seemed *exactly* that when Dina and I checked into the oasis of the Lotos Club on 17 December, for what would be a four-night, five-day stay. The people at the club were very nice about my not wearing a tie in the public rooms. This was strictly against club regulations, but when I explained why it would be impossible for me to comply, they made an exception. I felt no shame about playing the Cancer Card: we had theater tickets for three of the four nights, a dinner date with friends on one of them, and we planned to take Nina and Ana to *The Nutcracker* on Saturday afternoon.

I was looking forward to all of it.

EVAN'S PROSTHESIS HAS FAILED!

There was always the danger that this might happen. But it's always been easy to unblock mucus by sliding a brush inside the prosthesis and opening the channel. Now, a bit more than three months after it was installed, we have a larger problem. Every few hours, Evan needs me to help him clear the prosthesis. Even then, his voice lasts only a few minutes. And the moment we clear the prosthesis, it becomes blocked again. Finally, Evan loses his voice completely, and is forced to use the electro-larynx to communicate. I call Connie for help, and she gives us an appointment at once.

WHILE EVAN SITS IN THE examining chair, Connie and Dr. Stackpole hover above him asking questions . . .

'Are you feeling all right?'

'Have you been losing weight?'

'When did they last X-ray your chest?'

. . . and then, pointing to a swollen ring around the prosthesis, Dr. Stackpole tells Connie, 'There's granulation tissue here.'

I myself had noticed the formation of this ring, but I hadn't known it meant danger. They are obviously not pleased by this now. Dr. Stackpole tells Evan that she would like to talk to Dr. Harrison and Dr. Slavit, to arrange for an X-ray, and if necessary a CAT scan. I try to maintain my calm, but tears are already running down my cheeks. Joe Mulligan, the man who first gave us hope that Evan would speak again after losing his larynx, is there in the examination room with us, and he tries to calm me down.

Finally, it's decided that Evan will take the necessary tests. But meanwhile, they will have to remove the prosthesis. Evan will not be able to talk. In place of the prosthesis, they will insert a red rubber tube into the TEP, to protect his lungs from food or liquid leaking into them until the swelling goes down.

Evan asks if there's any way to avoid a red cable hanging down the front of his shirt; we are supposed to be going to the theater this evening.

They agree to take a chance on allowing him to wear a prosthesis that is really quite large for his TEP, so that the tissue will not become further irritated. Dr. Stackpole explains how dangerous it is to be messing around with the column, and prescribes medication to help the swelling go down, warning us to return at once if there is no improvement.

Evan is talking again when we leave the hospital.

IT WAS ONE THING TO be amiable and chatty in my own home with family and friends. It was quite another to be going to the theater for the first time since I'd had my throat slit, and then to a two-character play instead of a big noisy musical – an ill-advised choice, to be sure, but I'd made it myself.

Our seats were on the aisle. I sat on the outside. While Edie Falco and Stanley Tucci emoted quite marvelously onstage, I sat fearful that I would have a sudden coughing fit that would necessitate my popping up out of my seat and bolting up the aisle to the rear doors, upsetting the actors and the audience, and probably getting arrested for disturbing the peace.

No such thing happened.

I got through the entire performance without a single hack, and afterward Dina and I strolled crosstown to the Algonquin, where we sat in the lounge with two dozen other people, enjoying dessert and cappuccino.

The evening was a total success.

BACK AT THE LOTOS CLUB, while going through the usual nightly routine of cleaning Evan's prosthesis, I realized that it was hanging much looser, visibly looser, and it seemed to me that the swelling might be going down. It was difficult not to wake Evan at two in the morning to check on it again. I kept watching him in his sleep, and praying that he was okay.

By morning, there was no doubt that the swelling was going down.

We had arranged to take the necessary X-ray and CAT scans that afternoon.

We were looking forward to a pleasant evening out.

IN THE COP STORIES I write as Ed McBain, calling a perp by his first name is a way of letting him know that he has entered Copland, where you are the Cop and he is the Criminal, and you are in deep shit here. I am not in any deep shit here. True, there's some granulation tissue around the TEP, but we've changed the prosthesis, and the swelling's gone down and I had a swell time out on the town last night, and we're looking forward to another swell night out tonight.

So I'm not even bothered when at last I hear my first name called – 'Evan?' – and a white male Registered Nurse introduces himself as Tim or Tommy or Billy or Bob or Whoever with a Slurred Last Name. Perhaps he doesn't really mean to sound like it's four o'clock and he wants to go home, but that's the way he comes off when he says, 'Evan, have you ever had a CT scan before, and are you allergic to dye?'

He can see your throat, he has to know you've had a laryngectomy and therefore many CT scans before this one, but you tell him Yes, you've had many such scans, and No, you're not allergic to dye. 'Follow me,' he says, and before you can ask, he adds, 'Yes, she can come along.'

He takes both of you to a little windowless room at the end of a long cheerless corridor, and when you're both seated, he says, 'I'd like you to watch this video,' and without further preamble inserts a tape into a player, and pushes a button. A man who has never studied acting or public speaking introduces himself as Dr. Jones or Dr. Smith or Dr. Brown, and then goes on to explain that a CT scan utilizes X-rays to take highly sophisticated pictures of what's going on in your body, but that the level of radiation is less than you might encounter on any city street at any time of the day.

However . . .

However, there *are* certain risks if a patient is allergic to any of the components in the dye that will be injected intra-venously and there are risks as well that the dye may somehow be injected *under* the skin instead of into a vein, requiring surgery . . .

Surgery! I think. This is something new!

I'm only here for another CT scan! Will they have to amputate my arm?

221

. . . but these risks are rare.

'Nonetheless,' Dr. Jones says, 'because there *are* some remote risks, you will be asked to sign a release form indicating that you understand these risks and are willing to go ahead with the test. Thank you,' he says, and the tape ends without a fade-out.

'So?' the RN says. 'Did you understand all that?'

'Yes,' I say.

He moves a printed form in front of me. It is attached to a clipboard. In my experience with hospitals, I have learned that the patient is often asked the very same questions over and over again by a legion of doctors and nurses and technicians . . .

– 'Are you allergic to shellfish?'

– 'Are you allergic to any medications?'

– 'Do you have diabetes?'

– 'Do you have heart disease?'

– 'Will you please sign here, Evan?'

Bob becomes impatient when I begin reading what I've just been asked to sign. His disapproving look says, 'Didn't you just see the video, didn't you hear what I just explained to you, don't you *trust* us, Evan?'

I read the paragraph anyway.

It states that I understand the risks involved and am granting permission for the test.

I sign it.

'Come with me, please,' he says. 'You can wait here,' he tells Dina. 'This shouldn't take long.'

YOU ASK BOB TO BE careful inserting the IV because you have very difficult veins.

You are not just making idle chatter.

You have had blood drawn and IVs inserted on countless occasions, and have therefore acquired a sort of empirical knowledge about your veins. He listens as if he is paying close attention, but you somehow get the feeling he does not appreciate criticism in advance of the fact. He hasn't even swabbed your arm with alcohol yet, hasn't applied a tourniquet, hasn't slapped the arm to bring up the veins, so why are you telling him to be careful? Do you know how many IVs he inserts each and every day of the week? Relax, you're in safe hands.

But he sticks you once, and the vein either slips away or explodes, and when he sticks you a second time, in a spot higher up on the arm, the vein does the same thing again. There is a long silence as he ponders this peculiar circumstance. Patiently, you ask, 'Are you using a butterfly?' which is a very small needle, and he says, 'Yes, I am,' his tone bewildered now; how can this be happening to someone as experienced as he is?

Sometimes, even the doctors can't manage it; some of them haven't stuck a needle into a vein in ages. But the doctor Bob fetches gets into a vein on his first try. By then, I have a pair of puncture wounds in my arm, covered now with gauze and adhesive plaster, and I'm ready to suggest that we not take the pictures at all.

And even though I vow to take a firmer stand next time around (which in a Medland hospital can be every four hours) how can I ever hope to convince any nurse – *before* she sticks a needle into my arm two, three times – that my veins require very special attention? If she believes in her heart that she's seen my veins and others just like them a thousand times before, and knows exactly how to get into them, what else can I do but advise, explain, or even *warn*?

I have been here so many times now.

I have seen that totally astonished look cross a nurse's face as she realizes my veins are stubbornly refusing to support her conviction that she knows what she's doing.

I am so tired of it all.

I suddenly wonder how long this will all go on.

How long?

SUSAN BIRKENHEAD, AS YOU KNOW, is the lyricist for *Minsky's*. I had not seen her – or Charles Strouse, or Jerry Zaks, for that matter – since the day the Manhattan Theater Club people took us for a stroll through their newly acquired Biltmore Theater and promised (promises, promises!) that *Minsky's* would be the second show into their refurbished theater, after a straight play worked out the acoustical bugs. That had been early in 2002, months before the surgery.

For our one free non-theater night in the city, we'd asked Susan and her husband, the theatrical lawyer Jere Couture, to meet us for dinner. They chose a restaurant on the Upper West Side, close to their apartment on West 74th Street. The place was small, Italian, and noisy. The food was delicious, but the decibels were deafening. For most of the evening, I pulled my head back into my shell and scarcely said a word. When I did speak, I had to shout – and this broke the seal on the hands-free, which finally I tore off, ripping skin. For the rest of the dinner, I covered the stoma with my thumb and struggled mightily over the roar of the greasepaint, the smell of the crowd – but I made my voice heard.

I am told that in Shakespeare's time, 'voice of the turtle' meant 'voice of the turtledove'.

I wanted to go back to Connecticut.

WE STAYED IN THE CITY.

On Thursday night, we went to see *Imaginary Friends*.

Lousy, but no coughing.

On Friday morning, we got the X-ray and CAT scan results. No problems. And the swelling around the prosthesis continued to go down.

On Friday night, we went to see the revival of *Into the Woods*.

No coughing.

On Saturday afternoon, we took Ana and Nina to see *The Nutcracker* and were delighted by their delight.

We were back home in Connecticut that night, safe in our own beddie-byes.

ON 29 DECEMBER, JUST BEFORE the dawn of the new year (to coin a phrase), I sent this e-mail to Renaud Bombard in Paris:

> Cher Renaud: Well, I suppose you want to know if we're coming or not. Ecoute, mon ami. (Not for nothing am I the master of suspense.) We spent the week before Christmas in New York, attending the theater, dining out with friends. I was able to sit through every performance without coughing once, and I even managed to make myself heard in a very crowded, noisy restaurant. From December 23–28, we went up to an inn in Vermont where we spent the Christmas holiday with about two dozen other guests of the inn, engaging in lively conversations and even managing to joke about the device that enables me to speak. It still needs a bit of fine-tuning, but . . . well, I suppose you want to know if we're coming to Paris or not.
>
> Yes, we are coming to Paris. I don't think I'll be able to do any television, and even radio might be a little tricky, but I feel certain I can handle one-on-one interviews and even book signings if you want to arrange those. So, yes, yes, yes, book the hotel, book the airline and let us know whether or not to bring an umbrella. Oh . . . one other thing. No smoke-filled restaurants, please. The air I breathe is no longer filtered or warmed by my nose. Instead, it goes directly into my lungs. So if everybody's smoking, I'm inhaling all that stuff and that ain't good.
>
> Otherwise, we should be fine. Shall we give it a go?

This is what Renaud e-mailed back:

> Great, Evan! It won't be April in Paris, but February
> shouldn't be too bad, even though you'll probably need an
> umbrella. But don't bother to bring any, the Crillon will
> provide you with one (or even two!)
>
> Here's your schedule, tentatively . . .
>
> Arrival on Monday, Feb. 3rd, departure on Friday Feb.
> 7th.
>
> In between, not more than 6 interviews per day (starting
> on Tuesday 4th), which will all take place in your suite. A
> big cocktail party in your honor, with journalists,
> booksellers, publishers etc. on Wednesday 5th (also at the
> Crillon).
>
> No radio or TV interviews, except for one, if you agree to
> do it: the interviewer would be François Guérif (whom you
> know pretty well, according to my sources . . .) and your
> conversation would be taped, without any translation. It
> would be aired a few weeks after, with French subtitles. If
> you have any objection, please let us know and we'll cancel
> the thing.

And this was my response:

> Yes, Renaud, it all looks good, including the taped
> interview with François, whom I do indeed know well. I
> hope I'll be able to make myself heard over a cocktail
> crowd, but if not, Dragica will help me. We shall plan to
> leave NYC on February 2, correct? For arrival on the
> morning of February 3. Returning home on February 7.
> This begins to look very exciting. Paris! Ooo la la! Talk to
> you soon. Happy New Year to you and Sophie.

*

EVEN ON OUR DAILY DRIVE to the beach, I carry a small kit with me, containing the prosthesis brush, the surgical tweezers, extra sponge patches, the housing with its filter/moisturizer and a handful of saline ampoules. For overnight travel, we have a bag packed and ready at all times. It contains everything we need for daily maintenance.

But now we are about to travel abroad, and this is more complicated because of new airport security measures. Now we need special permission to bring the brush or the tweezers into the cabin. Now we must pack any sharp objects in our suitcases, both in mine and Evan's, in case one gets lost.

Before now, I have never been well organized. I used to rely on my husband to organize our trips, take care of our tickets, make sure we were sitting together – they often separated us because of my Slavic name. I wasn't even used to carrying a handbag. I knew that my husband always had his wallet with him and his driver's license. Sometimes I found myself having to call him to bail me out at the post office, when I realized in horror that I'd left my bag at Starbucks and could not buy stamps.

Now I carry a handbag with me at all times. Inside it is the soft, red rubber cable that must be inserted in place of Evan's prosthesis, in case this one fails too, and there are no nearby medical facilities. Without that rubber cable, everything my husband eats or drinks will leak into his lungs.

Now I try to be prepared.

ON 3 FEBRUARY, IN THE brand new year, we arrived in Paris at 8:50 A.M.

My first book tour since I'd had my larynx removed was about to begin.

*

IN THE HOURS ALLOTTED TO us for lunch each day, Dina and I strolled through a bleak, cold, gray beginning-of-February Paris. One afternoon, in the outside courtyard on the approach to the Louvre, we spotted a pair of young hoodlums trying to steal a Japanese tourist's purse. In my prosthetic voice, I yelled *'Vous!'* and pointed my forefinger at them the way I'd pointed it at the Nurse from Hell in my hospital room on the day after they stole my larynx. They ran away without the purse. But by shouting, I'd broken the seal holding the adhesive patch to my throat, and could only hiss all the way back to the hotel.

The seal broke only one other time, during the course of taping the *L'Express* interview late Thursday afternoon. I excused myself, went to the other part of the suite, and asked Dina to please help me put on a fresh one. When we returned, she explained that I would not be able to speak for the next ten minutes, while the silicone glue dried, after which the adhesive patch would be secure.

When I could speak again, I told François Busnel what had happened, and lifted the stoma cover to show him the plastic disc glued to my neck. Then I answered every question he had about the laryngectomy, and in a nation of diehard smokers – while the recording spools of tape unreeled – I dared to say that cigarettes had caused my present condition.

The next day, Dina and I had our very first fight since the surgery.

I HAVE HEARD SOME PEOPLE say that fighting is good for a marriage.

In my previous marriage, when my wife wasn't calling me a jackass in public, she was arguing vociferously with me about anything from politics to petunias, or even telling *People* magazine 'I think he's a bit crazy, but it's a psychosis well-channeled.' When she once told my then-publisher, 'Evan forgets things,' this precipitated a monumental fight because she could not understand that a writer's stock in trade was *remembering* things and you did not tell his publisher he was *forgetting* things! 'Besides,' she said, still unconvinced after we'd exhausted ourselves yelling on the streets of New York, 'you *do* forget things!'

By February of 2003, I'd been married to Dina for five years and four months, and if we'd had three arguments in all that time, I could not recall a fourth.

WE HAD A FOURTH THAT Friday, after the *Nouvel Observateur* interview.

Dina came back to the room after she'd spent some time shopping at Hermès, her favorite French boutique . . .

No, this isn't going to be that kind of story. This isn't going to be the husband exploding because his wife bought herself a new diamond ring or a sable coat. Dina's not that kind of woman.

But she had decided, after watching me confronting the hundred and twelve (it seemed) journalists who'd trotted through the suite in the past five days, that a stoma cover wasn't the proper neckwear for a writer of my stature. In much the same way that she'd decided 'a writer shouldn't have to work on a dining-room table', she had now decided that a writer shouldn't have to wear a polyester, Velcro-strapped patch of cloth on his neck, even if it *was* polka-dotted or paisleyed. So what she'd done was buy me two dozen silk ascots at a hundred and fifty Euros a pop!

Ascots!

I told Dina I was not Maurice Chevalier. I told her I had never worn an ascot in my *life*, and did not intend to start wearing one *now*. I told her I could never wear twenty-four ascots in the entire *rest* of my life. I told her that I didn't even know how to *tie* one, that anyway the silk was too bulky for me to reach under with my hand, that if ever I had to cough I would *choke* before I managed it, and besides we were *not* millionaires! €150 for a single tie came to whatever the hell $175 times twenty-four came to, something like four thousand dollars, was she out of her *mind*!

She began crying.

YOU SEE, I HAD NEVER got used to the look of the stoma cover. Even before we left for Paris, I'd begun my homework, making a list of everything I needed for Evan's new style. When I entered Hermès on Faubourg St. Honoré, I was well-prepared. A woman who'd helped me here on many occasions recognized me now, and I handed her my list. Shopping in Paris, in this luxury store, in this store that *specialized* in what I needed was frankly thrilling.

I chose large silk scarves lined with cashmere, one for each of Evan's winter coats, coordinating the colors. The ascots I chose to go with his winter sports jackets had to be in harmony with the scarves for his winter coats.

For his raincoats, I chose scarves without cashmere, so that they could be worn on warmer days, too. And the ascots for his lighter-weight jackets were all in brighter colors. I didn't need much for the summer. At a Giorgio Armani store in New York, I'd found shirts with collars cut high in a very imaginative way, perfectly suited to my husband's needs.

It was while all this was being packed, and my bill being prepared, that I noticed these very long, very beautiful silk scarves. They were not on my list, but I quickly realized they would make a nice addition to my husband's evening wear. I took a black one and a white one for black-tie events, and a pale blue one for his white linen suit.

I couldn't wait to go back to my sweetheart and show him everything I'd bought for him.

WE HAD ARRANGED WITH PRESSES de la Cité to stay at the Crillon on our own nickel for the next two days, planning to enjoy Paris and some family time with Sophie and Mark, hoping to do some shopping and to visit some galleries. I was exhausted after the whirlwind roundelay of journalists and photographers and Dina was equally exhausted, having spent much of the past three days in the bedroom part of the suite, rather than venturing out into the frankly forbidding winter streets of the city. And now, after having finally gone out to buy me some ties she thought I'd love, I was yelling at her, and she was crying – and *shit*! All I could think was if I had a larynx, I'd be able to wear a tie like every other man in the world, and I wouldn't be yelling at my wife whom I love more than anything else on earth, *shit*! Why did I ever have to get cancer, shit, piss, *fuck*!

I took her in my arms.

WE WENT OUT INTO A blustery cold Paris and returned a dozen of the ascots. Then we found a warm, cozy café, and we ordered cappuccinos with lots of foam, and that night we dined alone in a small French restaurant on l'Ile St. Louis, where Dina had lived for many years before she met me, and I held her hand tightly, and wondered for the hundredth time if she wouldn't have been much better off without me.

Successful tour or nor, I still wasn't there.

I still had a long way to go.

FROM JUNE OF 1996, WHEN we first began living together, to September of 1997, when we were married, Dina and I traveled to Milan and Venice and Florence and Sirmione. We went to Baltimore and Courmayeur and Jamaica and Barbuda. We went to Bangkok and Penang and Singapore and Yogykarta and Bali and Hong Kong. We went to Belgrade and Glavica and Vienna. We went to Oslo and Nottingham and London. We went to Cognac and Bratislava and Prague. We even went to Kenya. And then we went to Milan again, and to Venice for our wedding, and then to Mantova and to Portofino.

We were newlyweds, you see, and we had a lot of catching up to do.

Well, cancer caught up with us, and almost put an end to all that.

So now we had to start catching up all over again.

Paris simply marked a new beginning.

We had survived the journalists, we had survived the smoke-filled brasseries, we had even survived our fourth argument. On 26 February, we left for Sarasota, Florida, where we spent five days relaxing and resting with our friends Syd and Rita Adler, who without fail had visited Lenox Hill daily after the removal of my larynx.

On 12 March, I was in the city again as guest of honor at the 8th Anniversary of the Marymount Manhattan College Writing Center. It was a mild spring evening, and Dina and I walked in a leisurely way from the Lotos Club on East 66th Street to the Columbus Club on East 71st, where the ceremony would take place. I was wearing my hands-free valve, hoping it would get me through the evening. But within half an hour of our arrival, as invited guests began pouring into the club, the seal on the adhesive patch broke.

While I sputtered and hissed my hellos to other writers (and thankfully forgiving friends!) like Larry Block and Mary Higgins Clark and Michael Korda and Carol Higgins Clark and Roy Blount, Jr. and Nelson De Mille, Dina ran the five blocks back to the Lotos to pick up a new patch and the simpler HME valve, and then ran the five blocks back to the Columbus again, alarming Fifth Avenue doormen who kept calling after her, 'Are you all right, Miss?'

In the club's bathroom, we hastily repaired the patch.

Somehow, I got through the five-minute speech I'd prepared.

But it had been a close call.

At any future book signings – and none had yet been proposed by S&S – reading a chapter from a new book would take at least ten minutes.

I still did not think either adhesive patch would last that long.

ON 31 MARCH, WE LEFT for a four-day getaway to Cap Jaluca in the Caribbean. I watched Dina splashing in the sea, and I remembered a time not too long ago, when she sat on my shoulders at the K Club in Barbuda, and together, grinning, we braved each incoming wave. I watched her now, but I did not venture into the water.

I was afraid I would drown.

I had been told at the voice clinic that if just two tablespoons of water got into my stoma and down to my lungs, I would drown.

Two *tablespoons*?

ON 16 APRIL, I FINISHED *Alice in Jeopardy*, the first novel in a proposed new Ed McBain series, and Dina and I took a long weekend in the city. On 21 May, I finished an 87th Precinct novella titled *Merely Hate*, for a crime anthology I was editing, and two days later we were off again to Savannah, Beaufort and Charleston.

We were catching up.

On the third day of June, I began writing the book you are now reading. I had finished 186 pages of it when I drove Dina to the office of the Immigration and Naturalization Service in Hartford, to take her examination for United States citizenship. I sat outside in the waiting room after an examiner called her in. A Chinese man came out after just five minutes. A Mexican woman came out after seven minutes. A man with a Middle Eastern accent had to have been in there no longer than three minutes. Still no Dina. She's failed, I thought. They think she's a Serbian spy posing as the drama-coach wife of an American writer. Twenty minutes later, she came out beaming. The examiner had taken so long because she was questioning all those trips abroad we'd taken in 1996–97!

'I'll be sworn in sometime in October!' Dina told me. 'I'll be an American!'

Two days later, we left for Serbia to visit her mother and brother.

THE VILLAGE OF GLAVICA LIES some hundred and ten miles and two hours south of Belgrade. When little Dragica Dimitrijevic was growing up here, fewer than three hundred people lived in the village. Now, there are almost a thousand. When she was growing up, she and her twin brother used to stroll down to the river, hand in hand, to swim in sparkling clean water. Now the villagers dump their refuse in the river because ever since the war in 1999, there has been no garbage pickup. No one here in Glavica likes Clinton or Allbright. No one. No one here can understand why tiny Glavica was bombed.

Dragica can recall the village as it was.

There are still men walking by with wheelbarrows here. There are still horse-drawn carts and women wearing head scarves and carrying pitchforks. But now, there is a McDonald's in Paracin, the nearest big town, and you can buy Coca Cola here in the local grocery store. You can also buy drugs on any street corner.

We spend a full week with Mama and Dragan, my wife's twin brother. Family comes and goes, day and night, bringing food and flowers to welcome us. I learn some Serbian words and phrases. I learn how to say, '*Moja lepa Srbska žena,*' which means, 'My beautiful Serbian wife.'

Soon, I will have to say, '*Moja lepa žena*, Amerikanka.'

My beautiful *American* wife!

Soon, we will be leaving for the sea in the South of France.

I will not be able to go in the water.

I have a hole in my throat.

IF THERE IS ONE PLACE on earth I could choose for my paradise, it would be St. Jean Cap Ferrat. I love the charm of this coastal town in the South of France, with its villas nestled in lush gardens overlooking the sea. I love the quiet elegance of *La Voile D'Or*, and the breathtaking views from its terraced rooms. But most of all, I love its sophisticated flair, a quality hard to define yet unmistakably present.

After a two-year absence, Evan and I were going back there once again.

To rest and to relax.

To resume our lives.

IT WAS DINA WHO FIRST introduced me to St. Jean Cap Ferrat in August of the year 2000. We were supposed to go back there again in 2001, but had to cancel because of preparations for the September *Money, Money, Money* book tour, in itself cancelled after the Twin Tower attacks on 9/11. And last year, of course, we had to cancel yet again because I was recovering from throat surgery.

Recovering.

Ah, yes.

But . . .

If you'll never have a larynx again, how do you know *when* you've recovered?

If you can never, ever, for all eternity speak again without a prosthesis in your throat or an electro-larynx pressed to your neck, how can you ever feel fully 'recovered'?

I watch Dina splashing in the sea.

The last time we were here, we'd brought along our little Maltese poodle, Sasha. We bought a little inflatable rubber raft for him, and together Dina and I would push the raft from one of us to the other, little Sasha sitting in it, riding the waves like a happy, panting sea captain. He is not with us this time.

And Dina swims in the sea alone.

HEAVEN!

They know the special pastry I like for breakfast. They know how we like our beach chairs positioned. The bucket with our Evian water is kept replenished with ice. The umbrellas are moved to accommodate the moving sun. From our visit two years ago, they know we love cappuccino, and they bring it to us automatically at eleven each morning. At our favorite table, we lunch near the pool on the lower terrace facing the port with its sailboats and yachts. The raspberries are fresh from market, the cream whipped to a froth.

After lunch, when the sea becomes too rough, I prefer the pool on the upper terrace. The view there opens to the harbor below, the sky a clear blue canopy above us. Gigantic yews pierce the sky. The villas bask in the sun, shuttered to the heat outside. In the lazy afternoon at the end of the day, I swim my laps. A crawl to the far end of the pool. A breaststroke on the return. Evan sits in a lounge chair, watching me. He smiles as I approach. I smile back.

Our silent code.

I HAVE NOT DARED GOING into either of the hotel's pools. The one on the lower level, closest to the ocean, is too deep even to consider. The upstairs pool has a shallow end, but because of this it is favored by the children staying at the hotel, and I'm afraid some rambunctious eleven-year-old will inadvertently push me into the water. (Look, Mommy, the nice man is drowning!)

Dina goes upstairs every afternoon to swim laps, which she cannot do in the sea.

I sit in a lounge chair and watch her.

On one of these days, I observe a little boy in the water with his nanny. He is perhaps six years old. Seven maybe. I notice that he has no left hand. His left arm ends just above the wrist. When his nanny helps him out of the water, I see that his right leg ends just below the shin. He has no right foot.

He stands politely while the nanny fastens a prosthesis to his leg.

Equipped with an artificial foot now, he runs off shouting excitedly to where his mother is taking the sun at the other end of the pool.

Ten minutes later, I go into the water.

THERE ARE STEPS HERE AT this shallow end of the pool.

There is a handrail running down the center of the steps.

Here beside the pool, I've been wearing one of my little flesh-colored sponges to hide the stoma. I peel it off now. Dina is methodically swimming her laps. She stops at the shallow end. Watches me, as I grab the handrail and move onto the uppermost step. I sit on the steps. The water laps at my waist. Dina is still watching me. She moves closer as I step down into the pool. The water just touches my chest now. Some eight inches above that is the hole in my throat.

With my left hand, I grab for the tiles at the lip of the pool.

I take a deep breath.

With my right hand, I cover the stoma with my thumb.

I close my eyes, and duck my head under the water for just a second, surfacing again immediately.

'Okay?' Dina asks.

I nod.

I take another breath.

I cover the stoma with my thumb.

I close my eyes again.

I duck my head under again.

I surface again.

Dina is smiling at me.

I do it again.

This time, I am counting seconds the way I did while I was lying on that radiation table looking up at the monkeys in the blossoming trees painted on the ceiling, ah-*one*, ah-*two*, ah-*three*, ah-*four*, and I get all the way to twenty before I have to pop up to the surface to take another breath.

And guess what?

Nobody drowned.

I DON'T HAVE NIGHTMARES ABOUT losing Evan to cancer.

I used to have them quite often after his second heart attack. It was an almost-identical dream each time: We were separated by a crowd, and masses of people were pulling us further and further apart while desperately we reached for each other. We weren't yet married at the time, and my dream was probably a reflection of my daily waking nightmare: that one day, we wouldn't be lying together in eternal rest.

Neither Evan nor I are afraid of death. When we talk about it, it is with sadness, not fear. Yet, the memory of that morning, when I went for my last swim before our departure from Cap Ferrat, has never left me.

SHE WAS STANDING AT THE edge of the pool, adjusting her goggles, like a big bird against an already blue sky. She approached me gently. We exchanged good mornings and

238

expressed our good fortune at being in such a beautiful place on this sunny morning. Then she said:

'I was watching you yesterday. You love to swim.'

She paused for just a moment, and then knowingly and with precision, said:

'You swim alone.'

I faced her fully, waiting.

'My husband, too, had a laryngectomy,' she said.

In a calm voice, she proceeded to tell me about her husband, a painter, who was diagnosed with throat cancer and refused to give up smoking even when his vocal cords were gone and he could no longer talk . . .

'He painted all day with a lighted cigarette between his lips,' she said. 'I don't have a single picture of him without a cigarette burning in his hand or smoke filling his mouth. Was your husband a smoker?'

'Yes,' I said. 'But he stopped smoking long ago, at the time of his first heart attack. The problem with his vocal cords came soon after he quit.'

'My husband would not stop,' she told me. 'He did not want to go through the operation, because he did not want to stop smoking. When all was ravaged by cancer – his larynx, his esophagus – and he could no longer eat, or breathe, he finally let the doctors operate on him. Even then, while recovering from the operation, he tried to bribe the nurses to bring him cigarettes. He wanted to inhale smoke through his stoma. This is how addicted he was.'

Then very gently, almost as if she were whispering a secret:

'I know how you feel. Only the wife of a man who has gone through such a mutilation can understand the pain of such an operation. Because it *is* a mutilation, you can not call this horrible disfigurement anything else.'

It was more than a year since I'd thought about the loss of my husband's larynx as a mutilation. Since then, the word had left my perception of what we went through, to be replaced by a tenderness I feel toward this open space in my husband's throat, the intimacy I feel when I realize that this is how my husband breathes, the concern mixed with a genuine feeling of happiness each time I assist in the maintenance of what has become the most vulnerable part of my husband's body, a testament to what we endured together, a reminder of how lucky we are to have this life we share together.

'When did your husband have his operation?' she asked.

'A year ago.'

'This is when it comes back,' she said. 'After a year, my husband could not take food through his mouth any longer. They fed him through a tube in his stomach.'

I felt suddenly uneasy. I had not asked for this intimacy, and I wished that it hadn't been offered so freely. I looked at her. She was in her early sixties. Her face had beautiful bone structure, but the skin was a little too clear of blemishes, and the tightness betrayed a face lift. Her green eyes met mine.

'Six months after the cancer returned, he was dead,' she said, and then more gently, almost soothingly, 'I do not mean to frighten you. But what the doctors don't tell you is that the cancer *will* come back. After a year, after two years, it will claim the life of almost every other patient. You should know the odds.'

I felt suddenly trapped. I had no desire to argue numbers and compare survival rates with this stranger. Evan was doing fine, thank you. We had done everything we could do, taken all the precautions, and now we could look forward to a safe future. Fear of cancer was a memory we'd left behind, and I did not want this woman forcing me to look at a future we could not imagine. Evan and I were happy now. We were just ending the most wonderful, most romantic holiday, a holiday I would remember as my second honeymoon. I did not want my beautiful dream shattered.

Happy laughter came from the terrace, where guests were beginning to gather for breakfast.

'I must go,' I said. 'We have to pack, and we haven't had breakfast yet.' I turned away from her. 'Good day, madame,' I said, and walked away.

But even now I can feel her presence, as if she is still lurking close to me, her dark shadow casting its spell on my happiness. I have wished many times since our encounter, at the very end of a dream holiday, that she had never come to talk to me of death.

7

AND FOR MY NEXT
NUMBER . . .

ONCE UPON A TIME, LONG long ago, I visited China. We were among the first visitors from the West. Kids used to point their fingers at us and open their eyes wide. Look! Look! White skin! Round eyes! Blue eyes! Red hair! Blond hair! Look, Mama! Look!

Kids today know immediately there's something different about me. They don't point their fingers, but their eyes open wide when they spot the sponge patch or one of the valves covering the hole in my throat. Then, when they hear this gravelly voice of mine, they pay even closer attention.

This past summer, in the South of France, a little British kid – seven or eight years old, I guess – asked me, 'Why do you talk that way?'

I explained that I had no larynx.

He wanted to know what a larynx was.

I told him it was a voice box.

I told him I'd had cancer of the vocal cords.

I told him they'd had to remove my larynx, my voice box. I explained how I was now able to talk to him. I explained that I had this little doo-dad in my throat, and that when I covered the hole in my throat with my thumb, it forced air through the doo-dad, and I could talk to him.

'But you can understand everything I'm saying, can't you?' I asked.

'Oh yes,' he said, nodding. 'But how did you *get* this cancer?'

245

'I smoked cigarettes,' I said.

'I'll never smoke,' he said solemnly.

I STOLE MY FIRST PACK of cigarettes when I was fifteen years old. I had taken a summer job delivering groceries because I would be graduating from high school in January, and I needed money to rent a tux and buy flowers for my date and then go out on the town afterwards. We were so poor that . . .

How poor were you?

We were *soooo* poor that half the kids on my block didn't have larynxes.

Actually, we weren't so poor by the time I was fifteen. My father had struggled through the Depression as a 'substitute' letter carrier earning eight bucks a week, believe it or not, but now he was a 'regular', and we'd moved to the Bronx where we lived on a tree-lined street quite different from the one we'd lived on in East Harlem. I still had to earn money if I wanted to go to the prom, though, and the job I got was in Washington Heights, working as a delivery boy for a grocer named Ralph.

There were two other kids delivering groceries as well, Irish brothers named Tommy and Timmy Maguire, one of them sixteen, the other fourteen. They both smoked cigarettes. We would all three of us bring sandwiches to work with us, and on our lunch hour we'd go down to the basement where all the canned goods and bottles of soda were stacked, and we'd pop a Coke or a Pepsi to have with our sandwiches, and then the brothers Maguire would light up. I didn't smoke. I always politely refused when they offered me a cigarette.

You have to understand that back then nobody thought there was anything *wrong* with smoking. Nobody thought smoking could harm your health. Nobody thought smoking could give you cancer. Nobody thought smoking might

246

cause an aneurysm. Or a heart attack. So it wasn't that I was trying to avoid a bad habit that might cause sickness or death. It was simply that I didn't think I was *old* enough to smoke. Hell, everybody in my family smoked! My uncle and my aunts, my mother, all smoked cigarettes. My father smoked cigars. I just wasn't old enough.

I grew up the day I stole my first package of cigarettes.

We weren't the James Gang or the Daltons, you understand. We were just three kids in our early teens who were trying to get back at poor Ralph, whom we considered an old skinflint boss. We didn't even consider it stealing. It *was* stealing, of course, the same way opening those bottles of soda in the basement was stealing, but, hey, we weren't going into a bank with masks and guns, were we?

Here's the way the Great Robbery worked.

There was a row of shelves on the wall behind Ralph's counter. Groceries were stacked there. Also, on this same wall, opposite the cash register where Ralph could easily reach them, was a section where he stacked his rows of cigarette packs, Lucky Strikes and Camels, Pall Malls and Phillip Morris, Chesterfields and Kools, row upon row like wooden soldiers standing at attention. One of us – Tommy or Timmy or I myself – would casually stroll by the stacked cigarettes and knock two or three packs to the floor. Then Timmy or Tommy or I myself would come by with the broom and sweep them up, behind Ralph's back, down the aisle to the other end of the store where one of us would stuff the stolen treasures into his pocket.

The first day I smoked a cigarette, a twenty-year-old black maid in one of the Riverside Drive apartments where I delivered groceries, noticed I was left-handed and said with a wink, 'You owe a debt to the devil, boy.'

Sex and cigarettes would forevermore be linked in my mind.

Ciga-reetes and whus-kee and wild, wild women
They'll drive you crazy, they'll drive you insane . . .

That's the way the song went.

Didn't mention a word about all the other things cigarettes might do to you, but we didn't know.

We just didn't know.

THIS SPAM JUST ARRIVED BY E-MAIL:

CLICK HERE TO FIGHT NEW TAX INCREASES
Smokers 18 +
Don't miss your opportunity to help control state and government taxes imposed on the cigarettes that you purchase in the U.S.
CLICK HERE TO FIGHT NEW TAX INCREASES

They still don't know.

WHEN I WAS TWELVE YEARS old, I used to wow my parents and their friends by reciting from memory all of Abbott and Costello's *Who's on First?* routine.

When I was in high school, I memorized Edgar Allen Poe's *The Raven*, and I used to knock girls dead by reciting it to them flawlessly.

At Hunter College, I memorized *The Love Song of J. Alfred Prufrock*, and was similarly successful with easily impressed co-eds.

I joined the Powdered Wig Society, the school's drama group, and in plays like *Boy Meets Girl* and *Arsenic and Old Lace*, I played glib, fast-talking starring roles.

I had always had a smooth facility with words. Always ready with a wisecrack or a smart remark, I had charmed my way through childhood and adolescence, talked my way out of bar brawls and bad relationships, and had generally used words and wit the way some other boys and men might use fists and brawn.

Well, I can't talk my way out of this one because I no longer have a larynx.

Here's a hint:

If any enterprising network comes to you with an invitation to appear on a reality television show where they'll give you a million dollars in exchange for your larynx, tell them, 'No, thanks, I'll keep the larynx.'

Even two million.

Tell them no.

The larynx is better.

I've had a larynx, and now I have no larynx, and a larynx is better.

I truly miss my larynx.

I had my tonsils removed when I was seven or eight, and I do not miss them in the slightest. I *do* miss my larynx. And not only because it provided me with a voice and a certain social ease. That's the major part of it, of course, the inability to display my rapier wit at the drop of a plumed hat. The inability to flare up in anger. The inability to talk myself out of any given situation, threatening or otherwise. Without a real voice, I feel disenfranchised. I feel powerless. I feel frightened.

There are mornings when I wake up, and something or other is clogging the prosthesis, and I can't talk, and I'm suddenly reminded that I'm not a whole man. Something is missing. What's missing is my larynx. My voice box. I can kid myself that everything's okay, that the tiny vinyl disc in my esophagus is a perfectly acceptable substitute for a real larynx, but when it doesn't work – and it frequently doesn't work – I'm right back there on Reality Street. I do not have a larynx. I will never again have a larynx. I will never again have a natural voice.

One night recently, while Dina and I were watching a television show about UFOs, I said, 'Wouldn't it be nice if some aliens beamed me up and gave me a brand new larynx?'

And she held me close. And, no, there weren't fresh tears. We cried all those out the week we mourned the impending loss of my voice. But we came damn close. Because this had been a day that started with a clogged prosthesis when I woke up, and continued with my coughing up mucus all day long, and Dina having to poke a brush into the prosthesis each time it got stuck yet again, stopping me dead in my tracks as I struggled to get out a simple sentence, breaking the seal on the adhesive patch that holds in place the valve covering the hole in my throat, causing a hissing, puffing sound, but no voice, I do not have a voice, I will never again as long as I live have a voice.

And I start feeling sorry for myself all over again.

But that's not an option, you see.

AS I WRITE THIS, EVAN is expecting a live radio interview on the telephone. Fifteen minutes prior to the call, he gargles, and clears his throat. Then I come to clear the prosthesis one more time with the brush. We are both concerned, because it will be a forty-five minute interview, a very long time for someone with a prosthesis to be talking. Will the voice last? Will it become a gurgle? Will all this talking make him cough in the middle of a sentence?

We test the volume at which Evan can talk with the least pressure; it isn't very high, but they have microphones, after all, and technicians to adjust the volume on their end. As we wait for the call, my husband keeps bringing his thumb to the stoma, to test his voice. It's still there, but every time he tests it, he begins coughing. We check again for mucus. I come back with my brush. My husband looks at me and says, 'It isn't the same, is it?'

No, I think, it isn't the same, my honey. It will never be quite the same. The synthetic voice will replace the larynx my husband once had.

But we must learn to live with it.

And the message on the answering machine in our home is recorded in Evan's new voice.

ON 8 SEPTEMBER, WHEN WE returned from France, I went to see Harrison for my bi-monthly visit. Harrison this month, Slavit next month. That's the way it works.

He examined my throat, and said, 'I couldn't be more pleased with what I see. You won't have to come in again for four months. And you should schedule Slavit's next appointment for two months from now.'

Dina jumped out of her chair and rushed across the room to hug me.

'Am I still a cancer patient?' I asked Harrison.

'Yes,' he said. 'But you don't have cancer.'

'YOU CAN NEVER TURN YOUR back on cancer.'

Quote, unquote. Dr. Stanley M. Blaugrund.

'You can never trust anyone with a smile on his face and a loaded gun in his fist.'

Quote, unquote. Detective Stephen Louis Carella.

Same difference.

Cancer is a loaded gun.

I may not have cancer just now, right this minute, but I'll be a cancer patient for the next four years, at which time I will no longer have to visit Slavit and Harrison at all, at which time they can both safely say I'm cancer-free. If then. If ever. The overall five-year survivor rate for larynx cancer is about 68%. Better than the odds they gave my dear Mike Ockrent.

You can never turn your back on cancer.

In four years, I'll be eighty-one.

I'll have known Dina for twelve years. We'll have been married for almost ten of those years.

I want to live till I'm ninety-three. This may be an overly optimistic expectation, given longevity statistics. Just this past week, Herb Gardner died at sixty-eight, Althea Gibson and George Pimpton at seventy-six, and Donald O'Connor at seventy-eight. So maybe time is running out, cancer or no cancer. But P.G. Wodehouse, who shared my 15 October birthday, lived to be ninety-three, and he was working on a new novel when he died. That's my goal. Ninety-three, cancer-free, and still writing.

(Dina wants to know why not a *hundred* and three?)

I don't know how other going-on-seventy-seven-year-old men feel about themselves right now. Maybe they feel old. I hope not. I do know that despite everything that's happened to me, I do not feel like an old man, and I hope I do not look like an old man, and I certainly do not *think* like an old man, however an old man is supposed to think. In fact, I am still the 'well-developed, well-nourished, hoarse white male in no obvious acute distress' Dr. Strong described in his 1993 report, ten years ago, the very same man who met Dragica (*Drag* it, Sir) Dimitrijevic (Dim'me *T'ree* of Itch) in that Barnes & Noble bookstore fifteen months later. Who, by the way, will become Mrs. Yankee Doodle Dandy on October 16, the day after my seventy-seventh birthday. We have a lot to celebrate this year.

There is no Fountain of Youth, I know that.

We all die, and I'm getting there.

But the greatest battle I had to fight after losing my larynx was overcoming the sudden realization that I was not ageless. I said 'overcoming it', that's right. Not 'coming to terms with it', not 'accepting it', but overcoming it. *Feeling* young again. *Thinking* young again. *Being* young again. As young as I was on that January day in 1995 when I fell in love in a bookshop.

Methinks the lady doth protest, right?

The guy's seventy-six, almost seventy-seven, he's an old fart, toss him in the dustbin.

But I tell you, kiddies, inside every fat old lady you see waddling across the street rushing to catch a bus, there's still a sixteen-year-old girl in a yellow dress, dancing her heart out at her high school prom.

I will never turn my back on cancer.

But I'll never allow it to make me old, either.

I DON'T KNOW WHEN THE next book tour will be.

Or even *if* it will be.

When*ever* it will be, *if* it will be, I know I won't be able to manage it alone. Reading ten pages of a book aloud would be frankly impossible – even if I managed to invent a glue that would hold a valve to my throat for that long. So we've thought of my making a brief introduction, and then having Dina read the first chapter. How does that sound? She's a drama coach, she knows how to do that kind of thing. And how about hearing McBain with a Serbo-French accent? Then I'd do the Q&A afterwards, which I know for sure I can handle.

(Just now, as I typed this, I sneezed unexpectedly, bringing up fresh mucus. What if I sneeze during a Q&A? Gee, won't bringing up mucus simply delight my readers? My *former* readers, I should say.)

But I'm determined to do it.

I mean, what else can I do?

This is my job, this is my life.

Can I suddenly become a tap dancer?

You see, I realize that a spaceship isn't going to come down and change things in a blinding flash of light.

I have no larynx.

That's it, take it or leave it.

So I'd better take it, don't you think?

It's all I've got, Mom.

(Wanna hear me do *Who's On First?*)

THE OTHER NIGHT, I DREAMT I died.

Other people's dreams are usually as interesting as mud pies, but I think this one had something to say about recovery.

I was dead, no question about it.

A woman walked by with a big beautiful black cat.

She told me, 'He can't do anything but bark now, but he's all right.'

A black limousine pulled up, people all dressed in black inside. Dina got out of the limo. I put my arm around her. We walked together on the sidewalk. Just the two of us.

I said, 'I'm dead, you know.'

She said, 'I know.'

Sounds comical when I put it on paper now, but it was scary as hell, believe me. When I woke up, I lay on my back for a long while, feeling enormously tired, wondering if I might actually *be* dead.

I am no stranger to analysis. I once went to a shrink three days a week, for nine years, during which time I had to have written at least that many novels, plus short stories, plus screenplays, and God knows what. I later had occasion to call him for some information I needed, and he asked me at once, 'How's the writer's block coming along?'

But I did learn how to analyze dreams, and after I got over the initial shock of thinking I might actually be lying there dead, I tried to figure out what the dream meant.

You're ahead of me, I know.

The cat who could now only bark was me, of course, speaking through my prosthesis.

The man with his arm around Dina, alone on that sidewalk, was the me who once had been: The Man With A Larynx. I was telling her The Man With A Larynx was dead. And she was telling me she knew. But it was all right. The Man With A Larynx might indeed be dead, but The Man Without A Larynx was still very much alive. Sleek and strong, he might only be able to bark now, but he was still alive. He was still all right.

I figured maybe it was a happy dream, after all.

I'VE THOUGHT OF ANOTHER BLESSING.

The air I exhale comes directly from my lungs. It is always warm from the heat of my body. If ever Dina comes to bed with cold hands, I bring them to the stoma in my throat, and breathe gently on them, and warm them.

THERE IS A PUBLIC BEACH some twenty minutes from where we live. From 1 October through 31 March, we can take Sasha there and let him run free, off leash. Dina and I stroll up the beach with him, hand in hand, enjoying the changing tides and the swaying sea grass, the often churning waves, the seagulls swooping and diving overhead. Sasha pees on every piece of driftwood, every polished pebble, letting the universe know he was here. Sometimes, we'll sit on the huge rocks lining the shore, and watch the sunset. On days that are too cold for strolling, we'll sit in the car with the heater going, listening to classical music on the radio, watching for the sunset.

On one such day, we pulled into one of the parking spaces, and looked down at the beach, and saw that the shallow water was alive with white swans. We each counted them separately.

Dina counted twenty-five.

I counted twenty-five.

We each counted them again.

Twenty-five white swans were floating on the edge of the sea.

We didn't know where they'd come from or where they were going.

It seemed to us they were resting.

We figured they'd come a long distance, but still had a long way to go.

Holding hands, we sat watching them until the sun sank over the sea behind them.

Then we drove home, chatting excitedly about what a remarkable thing we'd just witnessed.

We were still talking about those twenty-five white swans when at last we fell asleep that night.